"Dr. Chapman has created a space to ask: Are we doing enough? Are we really helping? This book reminds us to see each child as a whole person, not just data or an end goal. It invites honest conversations about connection, belonging, and what's truly best for students. When kids feel valued, they grow. Every educator should read this."

Donna Jenkins, *Teacher, Deming NM*

"This book dares us to imagine what education could be if we truly centered children, families, and relationships. Through the lens of the superhero, it reveals how we can move beyond outdated systems and build something radically better, more human, more just, and more responsive. For those ready to shape the future of education, this is your invitation."

Tara C. Raines, *PhD, Deputy Director, Children's Advocacy Alliance, Nevada*

"I truly wish I'd had access to this book during my career. It highlights the challenges teachers and administrators face every day, and the impact of the choices we make. This book is a valuable resource and belongs in every classroom, giving educators practical, essential tools to better support students with special education needs."

Dr. Marvene Lobato, *Retired Superintendent, Fowler Elementary School District, Phoenix, Arizona*

"Parents and educators both agree that special education practices and student supports of the past are not working for students with complex social, emotional, and cognitive needs in classrooms today. Special Education Superheroes delivers real stories of students, teachers, and parents working together to create effective strategies helping to facilitate success socially and academically in the school environment. Superheroes is an enjoyable and easy read that makes the serious subject of special education relatable and interesting to all stakeholders."

Paige Engelnon, *Coordinator for Compliance & Professional Development, Arizona*

Special Education Superheroes

Special education is a strong framework for learning only when it is uplifted by teachers and parents who advocate for a truly inclusive system that is about unleashing potential, not overcoming disabilities. In this fun and powerful book, leading school psychologist Ovett Chapman offers easy-to-implement teaching practices that challenge the status quo special education system and move us toward inclusivity and personalized learning for all.

The book combines the author's real-world experience with evidence-based strategies and case studies, providing a blend of practical insights backed by current research. It shows you how to integrate new technology and collaborative approaches to craft more effective educational strategies, revealing that special education itself isn't the superhero – you are!

Special Education Superheroes is the ultimate guidebook for special education teachers, parents, and administrators who are working to create a future where special education is an integral part of an inclusive and dynamic educational system.

Ovett Chapman Jr., Ph.D. is an accomplished school psychologist with over a decade of experience serving children and families in public school districts. His expertise extends into the academic sphere as an adjunct instructor for graduate students in school psychology, where he blends in-depth theoretical knowledge with practical insights from his extensive professional experience.

Also Available from Routledge Eye on Education
www.routledge.com/k-12

Six Principles for Building a Truly Inclusive School:
A Call to Action for K–12 Leaders
Toni R. Barton

Tactile Tools for Social Emotional Learning: Activities
to Help Children Self-Regulate with SEL, PreK-5
Lori Reichel

Autism, Identity and Me: A Practical Workbook to Empower
Autistic Children and Young People Aged 10+
Rebecca Duffus, Lyric Rivera

Autism, Identity and Me: A Professional and Parent Guide to
Support a Positive Understanding of Autistic Identity
Rebecca Duffus, Lyric Rivera

Sexuality for All Abilities: Teaching and Discussing Sexual
Health in Special Education
Katie Thune, Molly Gage, Quinn Oteman

Supporting Your Child with Special Needs:
50 Fundamental Tools for Families
Rachel R. Jorgensen

Special Education Superheroes

Rethinking Conventional Practices to Best Serve All Students

Ovett Chapman Jr.

NEW YORK AND LONDON

Designed cover image: Getty Images/Yogysic

First published 2026
by Routledge
605 Third Avenue, New York, NY 10158

and by Routledge
4 Park Square, Milton Park, Abingdon, Oxon, OX14 4RN

Routledge is an imprint of the Taylor & Francis Group, an informa business

© 2026 Ovett Chapman Jr.

The right of Ovett Chapman Jr. to be identified as author of this work has been asserted in accordance with sections 77 and 78 of the Copyright, Designs and Patents Act 1988.

All rights reserved. No part of this book may be reprinted or reproduced or utilised in any form or by any electronic, mechanical, or other means, now known or hereafter invented, including photocopying and recording, or in any information storage or retrieval system, without permission in writing from the publishers.

For Product Safety Concerns and Information please contact our EU representative GPSR@taylorandfrancis.com. Taylor & Francis Verlag GmbH, Kaufingerstraße 24, 80331 München, Germany.

Trademark notice: Product or corporate names may be trademarks or registered trademarks, and are used only for identification and explanation without intent to infringe.

ISBN: 978-1-032-85239-3 (hbk)
ISBN: 978-1-032-85240-9 (pbk)
ISBN: 978-1-003-51725-2 (ebk)

DOI: 10.4324/9781003517252

Typeset in Palatino
by KnowledgeWorks Global Ltd.

Contents

About the Author viii
Preface. ix
Acknowledgement. xii

Introduction: Unmasking the Hero 1

1 The Misused Cape: When Labels Become
 a Costume. 10

2 Beyond the Mask: Each Student's Story 24

3 Sidekicks in the Classroom: Inclusion
 and Technology. 40

4 Redefining the Fortress of Solitude: Embracing
 Inclusive Environments 55

5 Justice for All: Culture, Identity, and the
 Inclusive Classroom. 71

6 The Power of Early Guardianship: Proactive
 Support for Future Heroes 86

7 Assembling the League: The Strength
 of Collaboration 102

8 Lifting the Signal: From Advocacy to Action 117

9 Beyond the Origin Story: Sustaining Change
 and Scaling Impact. 130

Conclusion: The Hero's Next Mission 144

About the Author

Dr. Ovett Chapman Jr. is a school psychologist, adjunct professor, and consultant with Wellspring Education Solutions. His work stays close to equity, mental health, and inclusion. Over the years, he has focused on building support systems that do more than respond, systems that see students' strengths before their labels. He earned his Ph.D. in School Psychology from the University of Arizona and remains active in the Arizona Association of School Psychologists, contributing wherever he can.

Through Wellspring, Dr. Chapman works with schools and districts to reevaluate practices that too often leave kids behind. A husband and father, he draws daily motivation from his own family and the belief that better schools are possible.

Preface

Why did I write this book?

It's a simple question, but the truest one I can start with. My favorite part of working in schools has never been the forms or the endless paperwork. It has always been the conversations.

Those conversations where you lose track of time. The ones with colleagues around a table, talking through what might help a student, or what a district could actually change if it meant kids would do better. Those long talks where ideas fly and people listen before deciding. That is the part of the work that has kept me coming back.

So I tried to shape this book like a conversation. As near to that as a book can get. The questions we toss around with the people we work with, the worries that keep us awake at night, the stories we tell each other because they remind us how important our work can be. That is where this book begins.

There is no shortage of new books talking about belonging in education right now. Some focus on frameworks, some on intersectionality, others on policy. Those are important topics and needed to push our field forward. Still, I have seen something left out of the discussion.

Too often, the voices of students fade into the background. The day-to-day realities, what kids feel, what they say, how they act when they know they belong, barely show up in these more polished frameworks. Instead, those frameworks sit apart from the day-to-day work of schools. No one stops to ask how those ideas hold up when you are sitting in a meeting trying to plan for a child with a complicated history.

I wanted a book that would start with those experiences. Students you might recognize from your own school.

Every story here comes from a real student. Their names have been changed, and other details adjusted so no one could identify them. The heart of these stories stays the same. Some were misread. Others were underestimated. Too many carried labels before they were even taught.

Their stories deserve room on the page. Because they force us to look again. They push us to question whether the labels we assign really help, or if those labels let us stop trying.

Special education has always been a complicated place. Labels, rules, protections, opportunities, all tangled together. But what happens when we look through the lens of belonging?

Belonging means a student does not have to prove they are worthy of support. It means they do not have to meet some artificial standard before we rethink how we work with them. From the start, they are seen and valued as part of the community, without needing to earn a place or prove they belong.

This book tries to make that idea sharper. To show how a strength-based perspective, along with a willingness to question old habits, can change what special education looks like day to day.

Alongside these stories, you will also see research. I have included studies, articles, and books to support these ideas. Research and data have their place, yet they need to stand next to what actually happens to kids.

If you are reading this as an educator, you will see the same frustrations you know well. The paperwork that can bury us. The quick decisions made at referral meetings. The plans that get filed away and never revisited.

If you are an administrator, you will see questions about whether the systems you oversee are set up to sort or to support.

If you are a family member, you might recognize the gaps between what your child needs and what the system is prepared to offer.

This is not a perfect guide. It does not present a step-by-step program. That is intentional. Conversations do not work like that, and neither does real change.

My hope is that you use this book the way you would use a conversation among trusted colleagues. As a place to wonder, to challenge, to rethink, to commit to trying something better.

There will always be a need for frameworks and policy guides. But there should also be space for stories, for actual experiences, and for questions that feel uncomfortable.

So why did I write this book? Because those long talks matter. They make us braver. They remind us who we are doing this for.

Most of us did not enter education expecting to be superheroes. We showed up because kids deserved better. We stayed when we saw how far small moments of support could go. This book is a way to honor those everyday moments of courage and stubborn hope that live in this work. That is its heart.

If we keep listening to students, families, and each other, we will see there is another way. That way puts belonging in the center. It does not have to sort kids by category. It keeps them in the circle, not outside of it.

I hope you will keep the conversation going.

Acknowledgement

To my wife and daughters, who are my reason for everything. Thank you, Monica, Callie, and Celeste, for making me a better person. To the many, many people who have talked with me, provided guidance, and made space for me to think. I appreciate you more than you will ever know. For all the kids whose stories drove endless conversations, may your stories continue to light the way for what needs to be seen.

Introduction

Unmasking the Hero

"Can you please tell us where she's going on Monday?" she said, gripping her husband's hand a little tighter. "We just bought her a new backpack. We want her to start school on the first day."

"Mr. and Mrs. Egan, I've been teaching kindergarten for over 20 years," the teacher replied. "In my experience, kids like Destiny tend to do better in our Autism program."

The specialist with the red hair adjusted her glasses and leaned forward. "Our program is designed for students who need more intensive support. Destiny's needs don't seem to rise to that level."

Mrs. Egan glanced around the room, searching for agreement. One administrator sighed and shook her head. Finally, the principal spoke. "Let's go ahead and start Destiny in the general education classroom. I think she'll be fine there."

That Friday afternoon, Destiny's parents sat in her Individualized Education Program (IEP) meeting, surrounded by a table full of professionals they'd never met. I imagine for them, the whole thing felt more technical than personal. They were new to this world of acronyms and evaluations, and it showed.

Do you know exactly what happened in that meeting? Probably not. Destiny's parents likely didn't either. That confusion, that subtle sense that things weren't adding up, is part of the point. Because for many families new to special education, this is how it begins: not with clarity, but with questions. With people speaking in terms you've never heard. With decisions that seem both urgent and vague. What you read wasn't meant to be neat. It wasn't meant to feel clear or resolved. It was supposed to be slightly off. That was certainly what it felt like to be in the room.

By the end of that meeting, there was a plan: on Monday, Destiny would strap on her new backpack and walk into her kindergarten class to join her friends.

But as the year progressed, Destiny's challenges became harder to ignore. Her limited verbal skills made social connection difficult. She often preferred to play alone. Sometimes she shut down completely, refusing directions or withdrawing from group activities. These were not simply signs of a student adjusting to school. They were symptoms of a deeper mismatch between her needs and the system meant to support her.

I have come to believe over the years that everyone in that room honestly believed they were doing the right thing. I was one of them. It felt like I was only minutes into my career and already making decisions that would shape a child's path. In retrospect, there are so many things I wish I'd asked, pushed, challenged. But like most of us early on, I deferred to the process. I trusted the system.

The truth is, our understanding of support was too narrow. We talked about placements, and we assigned services. We didn't ask enough about what Destiny actually needed to thrive. She had a one-on-one aide, which on paper sounded like the highest level of help. In practice, it often meant she was more observed than engaged. Present, but peripheral.

Maybe her teacher wasn't convinced she could succeed in that space. Maybe none of us were, really. Without that belief as a foundation, the rest felt hollow. Her IEP was legally sound. Her supports were in place. But Destiny stayed on the edges of the classroom, watching more than participating, included physically but not in experience. Her presence was more about compliance than connection.

Perhaps if Destiny had been paired with a peer buddy, had access to ongoing visual supports, or even a few scheduled sensory breaks, the classroom might have felt more like it was made for her too. While these strategies are simple and straightforward, when used purposefully, they signal to students that they are valued here. You're not an add-on. You're part of the class. When a classroom is set up with that in mind, students don't have to fight to belong. They can settle in, they can try, and they can learn. In a space like that, Destiny might not have just made it through the day.

Destiny's story is only one window into a much broader problem. What if we thought differently about the role of the educator? Not as someone expected to rescue or fix, but as someone who notices. Who adapts. Who sees what a student might need and makes room for it. These educators don't lean on programs or placements to do the heavy lifting. They ask better questions. They push past what's written in the file and start building trust, support, and connection. They don't do it alone. They collaborate with families, specialists, and other educators to build better systems for all kids, not only kids who are struggling. If more of us stopped and looked at how the current system operates and who it leaves behind, we might begin changing the conversation altogether. That's what unmasking the hero is about. Not stepping in with all the answers, but showing up with the courage to rethink the ones we've been given.

The system falls short in a lot of ways. But inside it, people are doing whatever they can to hold it together. In classrooms across the country, teachers are getting to school early to prep visuals, skipping lunch to finish IEP drafts, pulling colleagues aside to figure out what might actually help a kid. These efforts don't show up in policy briefs. They're not trending on social media or showing up in the latest research scan. But they matter. They're small, constant acts of care that keep things moving even when the structure itself can't keep up.

That kind of commitment is what holds schools together. It also makes it easy to believe we're already doing all we can. Most of us came into this work because we care. We've studied, trained, and reflected. We've sat through professional development sessions, read books, and stayed late to tweak lessons. And with that effort comes a sense of competence. We should feel like we know what we're doing. Sometimes, knowing a lot can make it harder to see what we've missed.

There's a study by Kruger and Dunning (1999) that gets at this idea. It showed that the less we know about something, the more likely we are to overestimate our understanding of it. This doesn't only apply to new teachers or overwhelmed staff. Even educators who've been at it a long time, who've found something that mostly works, can stop asking whether it still makes sense.

This isn't a judgment. It's a caution. Because in education, the stakes are too high to assume we've arrived. We all have blind spots. The moment we think we've got it all figured out is often the moment we stop asking better questions. The ones that lead to real change.

This kind of work deserves attention. Every day, educators show up with more than a plan. They bring the chance for something to change. Sometimes it's small. Letting a student choose how to show what they know. Giving someone a minute to breathe. Asking a different question. These choices don't always stand out. They can change how a student is treated. How they're talked about. Whether they get sent out of the room or pulled into the learning. A classroom doesn't need a total overhaul to feel different. Sometimes it starts with noticing what's been easy to miss.

Most of us got into this work because we believe school can make a difference. Behind every intervention, every progress note, every parent call, there's a hope that it can make a difference. That something we do might reach a student at the right time. Special education, at its best, is rooted in that same hope. Not as a system of labels and placements, but as a promise that no child will be left out of the learning community. It should be a structure that adapts to the learner, not the other way around.

Education should never be a tool for enforcing sameness. Its real power lies in helping students see the world clearly and ask hard questions about what they find. It shouldn't simply teach the rules. It should push students to question them. School should give students the language to speak up and the confidence to name what isn't working, especially in systems that have left them out or told the wrong story about who they are.

James Baldwin (1963) once said,

The purpose of education… is to create in a person the ability to look at the world for himself, to make his own decisions… To ask questions of the universe, and then learn to live with those questions, is the way he achieves his own identity.

He said this more than 60 years ago. The urgency still remains. Our work now is to help students figure out who they are. That doesn't happen by correcting them. It starts with how we see them, how we respond, and how we adjust. Every student has something worth bringing into the room.

Helping students understand who they are starts with what we notice. When classrooms are run in ways that listen more than label, we stop treating identity as a problem to solve. We give students a real chance to find out who they are on their own terms. That message shouldn't come once in a while. It should be part of how school feels every day.

As you move through these pages, consider this a pause. A chance to look closely at the systems we've come to accept. To ask what support really looks like, especially for students who've been overlooked, misread, or left out. This isn't about blame. It's about remembering why this work mattered enough to choose in the first place. Not for the paperwork. Not for the placement meetings. For the students who need us to get it right.

Big change takes time. But there are things that can start now: offering clear scaffolds, giving students different ways to show what they know, and making sure families are actually heard during IEP meetings. These may not feel dramatic, but they change the tone. They show students that they are worth noticing. That growth isn't just expected, it's within reach.

Still, it can't fall only on individual teachers. Lasting change depends on the system around the work. Time to plan together. Ongoing learning that connects to real decisions. Resources that aren't stuck behind red tape. Even in schools with limited funding, small actions can make a difference. When teachers have time to plan together or students get targeted support, those changes can start to move things in the right direction. Especially for students who have had the most taken from them.

When schools create time for this kind of collaboration, something changes. Educators stop feeling like they're doing all of it on their own, and trust builds. So does a sense of shared purpose. This work asks a lot. And when it's grounded in real connection, it reminds us what we're here to do. We didn't come to this field only to teach skills or evaluate students. We came to change what school can mean for every student who walks through the door.

Education is supposed to open doors. However, for many of our most vulnerable students, the path through school is lined with obstacles we created. When we talk about special education, we often think of it as a support. Something built to help. Too often, it becomes a barrier. Services get delayed or denied. Paperwork pulls attention away from people. Labels take the lead, while learning falls behind.

These problems don't show up the same way for every student. National data show that students of color are more likely to be identified for special education, placed in more restrictive settings, and disciplined more often than their white peers (National Center for Learning Disabilities, 2020). This isn't about ability. It reflects how the system responds to difference. That's who ends up paying the price. When race, disability status, or zip code determines access, special education stops being about support. It becomes another sorting mechanism.

This book is here to challenge that reality. It's about bringing the focus back to what actually makes a difference. How we build trust. How we make decisions. How we treat the students in front of us. Every student deserves to be understood for who they are, not managed based on a label. Not who the system has decided they are. Special education was never meant to separate students into categories. It was meant to make learning possible.

The journey is different for every learner. Yet our current model too often focuses on what needs to be fixed instead of what already exists. Diagnoses take center stage, and strengths get buried. We have to move away from a culture of correction and toward one of understanding. Special education is not about rescuing students. It is about clearing the way so they can move forward on their own terms.

This book is meant to be practical. Grounded in real classrooms and real experiences, it offers tools that can be used today. You'll find strategies that support inclusion, build stronger collaboration, and prioritize student-centered planning. These strategies aren't optional. They're part of what it takes to make sure students with disabilities are fully included in the learning.

At its core, this is about how we choose to see. It's about looking past limitations and recognizing the learner in front of us. The chapters ahead are a commitment to that perspective. One that honors difference, questions outdated practices, and pushes us to rethink how education is designed.

This isn't merely a story about inclusion or even about special education. It is a story about the limits of a system that was built with good intentions but not always the right tools. A system that too often treats support as a placement or a program instead of a practice. A system where labels are used to sort and separate, rather than to understand and empower.

That is what this book is here to challenge.

Because the heart of this work isn't about where a student sits or how much time they spend in general education. It is about how we think about differences, and the assumptions we make the moment a student is referred. It is about the paperwork, the meetings, and the checklists that sometimes take the place of real connection. It is about what happens when we stop asking what is wrong with the student and start asking what is not working in the environment.

We are going to talk about labels. About how they are used, misused, and sometimes weaponized. We are going to talk about collaboration, the kind that is messy, time-consuming, and absolutely essential. We are going to look at culture. At bias. At what it means to really listen to families who have spent years trying to make the system work for their child.

And yes, we will talk about inclusion. However, we will not stop there.

This is a book about reimagining what is possible. Not with magic solutions, but with real, human strategies. Strategies that come from classrooms, not only from textbooks. Ideas that grow from listening to students, not simply analyzing their data.

It's also true that we've made progress. Inclusion gets talked about a lot now. It shows up in conference sessions, planning meetings, and teacher prep courses. More people are starting to ask what it actually looks like in practice. Some schools are figuring it out. They've built strong co-teaching partnerships. They've used universal design to make lessons more accessible. They've adjusted how they do intervention to reflect real issues of equity and access. Across the field, there's growing attention to cultural context, overlapping identities, and giving students more say in their own learning.

But that kind of work isn't happening everywhere. And where it is, it's often too slow. Even so, it has a place. It shows what's possible when educators and leaders decide that inclusion isn't optional. When they stop making it something that applies only to a few students. It shows what's possible when educators and leaders refuse to settle for a system that only works for some.

> If you've ever sat in an IEP meeting and walked away unsure whether you helped or made things harder...
> If you've ever looked at a student's file and felt like the story inside it missed the most important parts...
> If you've ever wondered whether this system can actually do what it was meant to do...

You're in the right place.

> Let's unmask the myths.
> Let's rethink the roles.
> Let's get to work.

This is more than a book. It is a call to rethink what special education can be. Not a program, not a place, but a promise. Do not confuse this as a call for perfection. It's a call for presence. A call to recognize the impact you're already having and to imagine what's possible when that impact is supported by systems that work with you, not against you. When we unmask the hero within ourselves, we begin to shape schools that lift every student, not just the ones who already fit the mold.

References

Baldwin, J. (1963). *A talk to teachers.* http://www.elegantbrain.com/edu4/classes/readings/depository/race/bald_talk_teach.pdf

Kruger, J., & Dunning, D. (1999). *Unskilled and unaware of it: How difficulties in recognizing one's own incompetence lead to inflated self-assessments. Journal of Personality and Social Psychology, 77*(6), 1121–1134. https://doi.org/10.1037/0022-3514.77.6.1121

National Center for Learning Disabilities. (2020). *Significant disproportionality in special education: Current trends and actions for impact.* https://ncld.org/wp-content/uploads/2023/07/2020-NCLD-Disproportionality_Trends-and-Actions-for-Impact_FINAL-1.pdf

1

The Misused Cape

When Labels Become a Costume

To understand how special education works today, we have to look at how it started.

It didn't begin as part of the core system. It was added later. Created as a response to exclusion, and after too many students had already been left out. That history still shows up in how support is delivered and who gets seen as needing something separate.

W.E.B. Du Bois (1994) argued that education isn't limited to what happens inside classrooms. It's the full set of choices schools make about who deserves attention, what counts, and what gets ignored. Special education didn't come out of nowhere. It came from those choices.

I spoke with a retired teacher who began working in schools before there were laws for special education. Back then, there were no Individual Educational Programs (IEPs), and no formal process for identifying students with disabilities. Schools did what they could, or what they thought they had to. She told me about a student named Kevin, who asked a lot of questions, moved around constantly, and talked when he wasn't supposed to. The staff didn't know how to support him. They saw him as a problem. Over time, he stopped showing up.

There was no meeting, no plan, and no one called home. He disappeared from school, and no one followed up. She still remembered him. Kevin wasn't the only one. He was one of many. Special education didn't erase those stories. But it made them harder to ignore.

How We Got This Cape

From the start, public education focused on certain students. Others were left out, not always by design, but often by the way the system defined who belonged. As Rufo and Causton (2021) explain, schools were organized around a narrow idea of who could succeed. Students who didn't match that picture, especially those with disabilities, were excluded or placed on separate tracks that rarely led back into those schools.

By the time special education came along, the structure was already in place. General education had been defined, standardized, and protected. Support for students who didn't fit that structure wasn't created from the beginning. It was added later. What we now call "services" started as a separate track, not a plan for full inclusion.

Winzer (2009) describes early public schooling as rigid, one-size-fits-all, and organized to produce conformity. Students were grouped, labeled, and judged by their ability to meet predefined norms. Those who couldn't keep up were seen as problems to be fixed or removed. There was no mechanism for adapting instruction or rethinking expectations. The system wasn't broken. It was working exactly as intended.

So when special education entered the picture, it didn't reshape the structure. It worked around it. Programs were created to serve students with disabilities, but the underlying design stayed the same. The message was clear: support would be provided, but only from the outside.

Before the Law: Separation, Labels, and Denial

Long before there were legal protections, schools had already decided who belonged. In the 19th and early 20th centuries, children with disabilities were often labeled uneducable. That wasn't only a perception, it was policy. Many states had laws on the books that excluded students based on disability, behavior, or assumed capacity to learn (Winzer, 2009). Entire categories of children were shut out.

The few options that did exist weren't educational in any meaningful sense. Some children were sent to asylums or custodial institutions. Others ended up in charity-run programs with limited access to instruction. These were not schools in the way most people would define them. They were holding places. The goal was supervision, not learning (Lengyel & VanBergeijk, 2021).

Elizabeth Farrell pushed against that. She was a teacher in New York City who began working with students who had been written off by the system. In 1899, she created one of the first public school classes for what were then called "backward children." She advocated for individualized teaching and believed that every student could learn (Winzer, 2009). Her work marked a change, not only in practice but in how educators thought about students with disabilities.

Still, Farrell's model didn't disrupt the larger structure. It worked within it. These special classes were physically separate. They had their own teachers, their own schedules, and their own rules. The students were still apart. The system hadn't made room for them. It had simply moved them out of the way.

These early efforts were framed as progress. Compared to total exclusion, they were. But they also made something else harder to question. Once separate tracks were created, they became the default. The idea that students with disabilities needed to be somewhere else shaped how schools operated. And that idea stayed in place, even as the labels and laws evolved (Yell et al., 2011).

Brown Didn't Mention Disability, But It Changed Everything

Brown v. Board of Education (1954) forced schools to face something they had long ignored. The United States Supreme Court ruled that separating students by race was not equal, not fair, and not legal. Disability wasn't part of that case, but the ruling made one thing harder to defend: the idea that it was acceptable to separate some students from the rest and call it support.

Families of children with disabilities who had been told their children couldn't go to school started asking harder questions. Some of these families had been told to keep their kids at home, while others had been directed to institutions. There were no meetings, no paperwork, and no talks about next steps. The school simply said no and moved on.

Brown didn't necessarily solve that problem, but it gave families a reason to come back to the table. It gave them a legal argument, not just a moral one. In the years that followed, parents across the country began to use that argument to challenge how schools treated students with disabilities. Those cases didn't just open doors. They laid the foundation for the laws that came next.

The Parents Took It to Court

By the early 1970s, too many families had heard the same answers: no placement, no services, and no space. Some districts offered referrals to programs that didn't exist or pointed to waitlists that never moved, and others gave no explanation at all. The message was clear: if your child couldn't walk, talk, focus, or learn the way the school expected, they were someone else's responsibility. So families went to court.

In Pennsylvania, a group of parents came together through the Pennsylvania Association for Retarded Citizens (PARC). They filed a class action suit against the state. Their children had been denied access to school solely because of their disabilities. The case, *PARC v. Pennsylvania* (1971), ended with a consent decree that changed everything. The court recognized that children with intellectual disabilities had a constitutional right to a public education (Yell et al., 2011). This was not a bonus or a favor, but a right.

A year later, in the District of Columbia, another group of families sued the school system for denying services based on lack of funds. Their children had been removed from classrooms or quietly pushed aside when budgets got tight. In *Mills v. Board of Education* (1972), the court ruled that public education couldn't be offered to some and withheld from others. If the school doors were open, they had to be open for every student (Lengyel & VanBergeijk, 2021).

These cases didn't fix the system, but they changed what families could demand. They introduced principles that still shape special education law: the right to a public education, the refusal to reject any student, and the need for written plans and due process when schools fall short. None of these were technical terms at the time. They were responses to real harm.

Even as those protections were written into law, the structure of separation stayed in place. Rufo and Causton (2021) point out that schools still use labels and placements to decide what kind of support a student gets. Instead of asking what a student needs, the system looks at the diagnosis first. Help isn't something every student can get when they need it. It's something you have to qualify for.

The Law Arrives and Starts to Change

When the Education for All Handicapped Children Act was passed in 1975, schools were no longer allowed to turn students away. Families didn't have to beg for access or take whatever scraps a district might offer. The law made it clear that students with disabilities had a right to be there. That didn't mean the system was ready.

Schools were told to create something they had never done before. Suddenly, there was a requirement for individualized education programs. Support had to happen in the least restrictive environment. Evaluations needed to be fair, and families had to have a real voice in decisions. These ideas weren't new to parents, but they were new to policy. Meanwhile, while the law gave families leverage, it left schools with very little clarity on how to make any of it work.

What counted as "appropriate" education became the next fight. In *Board of Education v. Rowley* (1982), the Supreme Court said schools had to provide services that were reasonably calculated to help a student make educational progress. But the ruling didn't spell out what progress should look like. Over time, that gap left room for interpretation. Courts often accepted plans that showed minimal growth. Some even described the standard this way: schools didn't have to provide a Cadillac, just a serviceable vehicle that got the student down the road. That reasoning stuck around for decades until another case asked whether getting down the road was really enough.

Other court cases filled in the blanks. In *Honig v. Doe* (1988), schools were told they couldn't remove students for behavior tied to their disability. In *Timothy W. v. Rochester* (1989), a district had argued that a student was too disabled to benefit from school at all. The court disagreed. No matter the severity, students had the right to be educated.

Over time, the law changed names and added pieces, including early intervention, transition services, functional behavioral assessments, and postsecondary planning. These additions came in waves, starting in 1990, then again in 1997, and once more in 2004, as families kept pushing and schools kept falling short.

Then came *Endrew F.* (2017). The Supreme Court revisited the standard first set by *Rowley* and made it harder to defend low expectations. Schools could no longer settle for plans that offered minimal benefit. IEPs had to be "reasonably calculated" to help students make meaningful progress, not just any progress. It wasn't about providing the Cadillac, but it did mean the car had to run well enough to get somewhere that mattered. Goals had to be ambitious enough to reflect the student's potential, not written to match the system's limitations.

Each version of the law added something. It didn't, however, change the fact that most schools were trying to build new systems on top of old ones. The foundation was still the same.

The Movement Behind the Law

Change didn't start in the courtroom. It started with people who were tired of being told no. Some of them were parents. Some were students. Many were disabled adults who had already lived what the system tried to deny.

Judith Heumann had been blocked from becoming a teacher because she used a wheelchair. This was not due to the idea she couldn't teach, but because the city said she was a fire hazard. She took the case to court and won. Then she kept pushing. In 1977, she helped organize the sit-in at the San Francisco office of Health, Education, and Welfare. Protesters occupied the building for nearly a month, refusing to leave until Section 504 of the Rehabilitation Act was enforced (Ladau, 2021; Lengyel & VanBergeijk, 2021).

Bradley Lomax was there too. He was a wheelchair user and a member of the Black Panthers. The Panthers brought food and stayed with the protesters. They didn't show up out of charity. They showed up because they understood what it meant to be shut out of public systems. Disability rights and racial justice weren't separate fights (Ladau, 2021).

That same energy showed up in other places. Eunice Kennedy Shriver started the Special Olympics in 1968 to give athletes with intellectual disabilities a place to compete and be seen. They weren't there to inspire anyone or to be pitied. They were there because they belonged (Ladau, 2021).

The documentary *Crip Camp* (LeBrecht & Newnham, 2020) shows what that work looked like up close. Young people with disabilities learning how to organize, speak up, and fight back. Nothing about it was easy, and none of it was handed over.

A Law Can't Do the Work Alone

Individuals with Disabilities Education Act (IDEA) promised students with disabilities the support they needed to learn. That only worked if schools had the funding, training, and time to follow through. It also required leaders willing to change how schools worked.

The law says students should be taught in the least restrictive environment. That's been written into federal policy for decades. Still, across the country, many students spend most of their school day in separate classrooms. Some are pulled out for services. Others are placed in entirely different programs, far from their peers. The placement decisions may be legal, but that doesn't make them right.

Legal protections gave families something to point to. They gave them leverage when schools refused to listen. Having rights on paper didn't stop schools from pushing back. For every student who gained access because of IDEA, there are others whose families had to fight their way through meetings, appeals, and legal battles just to get basic support (Yell et al., 2011).

Compliance is not the same as commitment. It's possible to follow the rules and still miss the point. IEPs can be written and delivered exactly as required, while the student sits in a room that no one else visits. Services can be provided on schedule, even if no one ever asks whether they're working.

This isn't the first time it's been said, and it won't be the last: special education wasn't part of how schools were originally organized. It was added after the fact, designed to support students the system hadn't planned for. That separation didn't end with legislation. It still shows up in how students are placed, when services are delivered, and how support gets described.

Rufo and Causton (2021) describe this as one of the field's core contradictions. Services are often locked behind eligibility gates, even when students clearly need help. This turns special education into a gatekeeper, not a flexible system of support. It ends up reinforcing the very barriers it should serve to break down.

Where History Leaves Us

The history of special education is often told as a story of progress. We are familiar with the court cases, laws, and expanded rights. While that part is true, it's not the whole story. Progress has always come with pushback. Every gain has had to be defended, again and again.

The same system that once locked students out now labels them in. Students are included on paper but set apart in practice. Services are offered, but often in ways that reinforce difference instead of challenging the structures that make learning harder in the first place.

The core question hasn't gone away. Do we want special education to be a system of support? Or a system of separation? That question shows up every day in how teams make placement decisions, how IEPs are written, and how students get sorted into programs based on assumptions about where they belong.

Laws can guarantee access. They can force schools to open their doors. What they can't do is guarantee connection. They can't make a team listen. They can't rewrite how people see a student before they even walk into the room.

This history isn't something to admire. For every student caught in a system that says one thing and does another, we have to ask ourselves something simple: are we really including them, or are we simply doing the paperwork?

Rethinking Our Approach

Despite everything that's been written into law, special education still carries the marks of the system that shaped it. IDEA helped open doors, but it didn't guarantee what would happen after a student walked through. The supports are supposed to be there. So are the learning environments. Too often, they aren't.

The numbers tell part of the story. The graduation rate for students with disabilities sits around 71%. For all students, it's closer to 87% (National Center for Education Statistics [NCES], 2022). That gap isn't new, and it isn't random. It comes from years of assumptions, underfunded services, and decisions that limit access in the name of support.

Students with disabilities are more than twice as likely not to graduate on time. The reasons vary, but the pattern doesn't. IEPs get written, accommodations are listed, and meetings are held. None of that guarantees students will get what they actually need. Too often, they're placed on modified tracks that expect less, teach less, and offer fewer ways back in. Instead of changing how schools work, the system changes what we expect from the student.

The problem is not usually a lack of will. Most educators care about their students. They want to support all students, but intention is not the same as capacity. Without time to collaborate, access to specialists, or professional development focused on inclusive strategies, even the most committed teachers can feel overwhelmed. Special education becomes something separate, something handled "over there" by someone else. Students with IEPs are pulled out for services, pushed into modified tasks, or passed along the system without ever being fully understood.

All of this reveals a deeper problem. At its core, the system remains anchored to a deficit model. We identify what is "wrong" with the student, list their areas of weakness, and build a plan around managing those deficits. This approach might help with compliance, but it does little to nurture potential. It tells students what they can't do before exploring what they can.

The irony is that we already know better. Research has shown for years that when schools focus on what students can do, engagement improves, confidence grows, and outcomes follow. That does not mean ignoring challenges. It means starting from a real understanding of the student rather than a list of deficits.

Labels don't exist on their own. They come from a way of thinking about disability. That thinking shapes how we plan, how we place, and how we talk. For much of its history, special education has followed the medical model of disability, which treats disability as something inside the student that needs to be corrected. Under that model, the job is to diagnose, fix, and get the student to function more like their peers. That's where we get service minutes, eligibility criteria, and the idea that students with certain labels belong somewhere else. You see it even in well regarded resources like *The IEP Checklist* (Rosas & Winterman, 2023), where planning starts with identifying needs and aligning services, usually after a label has been applied. That sequence is built on the belief and practice that support comes after we identify something wrong.

In 2022–2023, 7.5 million students ages 3–21 received special education services under IDEA. That's about 15% of all public school students (NCES, 2024). The most common disability category was specific learning disabilities, making up nearly a third of those served. But having an IEP doesn't guarantee real support. Services can be inconsistent. Missed sessions, unmet accommodations, and overworked staff all play a role. Sometimes it's a staffing issue. Sometimes it's logistics. Either way, the student pays the price.

The way we think about disability shapes everything else. How we write goals. How we measure progress. How we talk about what's possible. Even when schools mean well, many practices still reflect an old mindset: one that treats disability as something to manage or fix. That way of thinking didn't disappear. It shows up in how we track services, how we place students, and how we define success. These are not abstract ideas. They affect what students experience every day.

Inclusion doesn't come from filling out the right forms. It comes from how classrooms are structured. Who the lessons are designed for. Whether students feel like they belong. Whether teachers have the tools to respond to difference without sending students somewhere else.

Success shouldn't be about how closely a student can match their peers. That lens is far too narrow. When we expand how learning can be demonstrated, we change who gets seen, who gets credited, and who gets believed.

Special education is often seen as the solution. The safety net if you will. The system that steps in when everything else has been tried. We use it to "catch" students who are falling behind, to offer support when general education can't stretch any further, and to reassure families that their child is being helped. In that way, special education becomes the cape. It swoops in, offers rescue, and promises protection.

But capes don't just symbolize help. They can also reinforce the idea that someone needs saving in the first place.

When we frame special education as the heroic fix, we risk creating a story where the student is always in need of rescue and the system is always the answer. And while that story might come from a place of care, it also lets the rest of us off the hook. If special education is where support lives, what does that mean for general education? For core instruction? For school culture? If the cape is always the solution, then we stop looking for ways to make the whole system more responsive.

This mindset doesn't only put pressure on students. It puts pressure on special educators too. They're often expected to solve complex challenges in isolation: navigating behavior, academic gaps, service delivery, and emotional labor with limited time or collaboration. At the same time, general educators may believe that once a student has an IEP, the responsibility shifts away from them. Not out of malice, but out of habit. And that habit keeps us stuck.

It also puts pressure on the system itself. Special education, while essential, was never meant to be the only engine of support. Yet it's often treated that way. Reading interventions that should happen in Tier 1 get pushed into special ed. Behavioral concerns that stem from trauma, language barriers, or classroom mismatch are routed into referral pipelines. We begin to treat special education not merely as a service, but as the place where students go when we've run out of other ideas.

In this way, the cape becomes a shortcut. It covers up instructional gaps, avoids deeper conversations about bias or expectations, and lets systems keep operating without change. And most importantly, it limits our imagination about what students are capable of when given the right conditions from the start.

This book isn't an argument against special education. It's an argument against over-reliance. Against the idea that one system, one label, or one team can be responsible for everything a student needs. The superhero metaphor works when it reminds us of the courage and care it takes to support students well. But it breaks down when we act like special education is the only place that work should happen. General education teachers are with students every day. They build the relationships, teach the content, and make the small decisions that shape whether a student is included or left out. Support can't sit in the hands of a few. Real impact happens when we stop waiting for rescue and start building better systems together.

We're not starting from scratch. We're working in a system that's been shaped by years of advocacy, legal pressure, and lived experience. Some of that has led to real progress. Some of it has led to practices we're still trying to undo. The gaps in graduation and support didn't come out of nowhere. They reflect how the system still works and what it continues to miss.

This chapter does not offer a simple solution, nor does this book. There isn't one simple solution. What it does offer is a reason to stop and ask the harder questions. Are we creating systems that adapt to students? Or are we still asking students to adapt to the system? Are we using special education to empower, or just to contain?

The answers won't be the same everywhere. They'll depend on the district, the building, and the people in the room. What is imperative is that we keep asking the questions. They help us step back from what we've come to accept. They remind us that the system is shaped every day by the choices we make: what we write in referrals, how we lead meetings, and how we talk about the students in front of us.

If special education has become the cape we reach for, then we have to ask what we're trying to protect students from. Chapter 2 begins that work by turning our attention to the label itself. Not to define the student, but to look at what the label has come to represent. If we want something better, we have to be honest about how the label has been used and be willing to see the student who's been there all along.

References

Board of Education of the Hendrick Hudson Central School District v. Rowley, 458 U.S. 176 (1982).

Brown v. Board of Education, 347 U.S. 483 (1954).

Du Bois, W. E. B. (1994). *The souls of black folk*. Dover Publications. (Original work published 1903)

Endrew F. v. Douglas County School District RE-1, 580 U.S. 386 (2017).

Honig v. Doe, 484 U.S. 305 (1988).

Ladau, E. (2021). *Demystifying disability: What to know, what to say, and how to be an ally*. Ten Speed Press.

LeBrecht, J., & Newnham, N. (Directors). (2020). *Crip camp: A disability revolution* [Film]. Higher Ground Productions; Netflix.

Lengyel, L. S., & VanBergeijk, E. (2021, June & July). A brief history of special education: Milestones in the first 50 years [Parts 1 & 2]. *EP Magazine*. https://epmagazine.com

Mills v. Board of Education of District of Columbia, 348 F. Supp. 866 (D.D.C. 1972).

National Center for Education Statistics. (2022). *Public high school graduation rates*. U.S. Department of Education, Institute of Education Sciences. https://nces.ed.gov/programs/coe/indicator/coi

National Center for Education Statistics. (2024). *Students with disabilities* (The Condition of Education 2024). U.S. Department of Education, Institute of Education Sciences. https://nces.ed.gov/programs/coe/indicator/cga

PARC v. Commonwealth of Pennsylvania, 343 F. Supp. 279 (E.D. Pa. 1971).

Rosas, C. E., & Winterman, K. G. (2023). *The IEP checklist: Your guide to creating meaningful and compliant IEPs* (2nd ed.). Brookes Publishing.

Rufo, J. M., & Causton, J. (2021). *Reimagining special education: Using inclusion as a framework to build equity and support all students* (1st ed.). Brookes Publishing.

Timothy W. v. Rochester, New Hampshire, School District, 875 F.2d 954 (1st Cir. 1989).

Winzer, M. A. (2009). *From integration to inclusion: A history of special education in the 20th century*. Gallaudet University Press.

Yell, M. L., Katsiyannis, A., & Bradley, M. R. (2011). The Individuals with Disabilities Education Act: The evolution of special education law. In J. M. Kauffman & D. P. Hallahan (Eds.), *Handbook of special education* (pp. 61–76). Routledge.

2

Beyond the Mask

Each Student's Story

"I don't know what we're going to do with this student." The principal looked tired. We were reviewing paperwork on a new transfer, Jordan. Labeled with an emotional disability since elementary school. The file was overflowing with incident reports, suspensions, and school transfers. It read more like a warning than a history, and it was hard to look past.

Jordan didn't offer much. You could go weeks without more than a nod or a sentence. When we tried to connect, he pulled back. This was not him being resistant, nor was it hostility. He had learned how to keep his distance. Whatever he'd been through before us, it had taught him to stay guarded.

After another incident, he was placed in a private day school. The director told me Jordan's first week was unremarkable. He came in, followed directions, and made it through the day. Nothing close to what we'd expected. "We gave him time," the director said. "Paid attention." That slower pace and fewer assumptions worked. It should be common, yet it rarely is.

Erving Goffman (1963) called it a "spoiled identity." When the label starts talking before the student has a chance to. That's what happened with Jordan. By the time he got to us, most people had already made up their minds. They'd read the file and heard the warnings. People met the label before they met him. And once that happens, it takes real work to see what's still there.

The Purpose and Pitfalls of Labels

Labels are supposed to help. That's how they're explained, at least. A way to open doors. Get students access to support. Under Individuals with Disabilities Education Act (IDEA), schools are required to categorize (Individuals with Disabilities Education Act, 2004). A name goes in a box, and with that box comes services. That's the structure.

But labels don't stay on the paperwork.

They show up in meetings, side comments, and placement decisions. They influence how a student gets introduced. And once they're there, they tend to stay.

Algozzine et al. (1977) found what many educators already knew. Students with behavior labels were often treated based on category, not conduct. The label came first, then the reaction. That pattern is still with us. Expectations drop. The way we respond changes.

Jordan didn't enter schools as a student. He showed up as a file. His label didn't just follow him; it preceded him. People were already preparing for how they thought he would act.

Rosenthal and Jacobson (1968) showed how quickly adult beliefs can shape student outcomes. Lower expectations lead to fewer chances. Fewer chances lead to fewer results. The cycle reinforces itself.

Some labels do help. They give teams language, guide planning, and clarify needs. But many don't. They're rushed, unclear, or used as shorthand for behavior. Over time, the label stops being a tool and starts defining the student.

Skrtic (1991) called this the special education paradox. A system designed to provide support ends up reinforcing separation. Services are tied to categories. If you don't fit, you don't get in.

Inclusion doesn't begin with eligibility. It begins when we stop measuring students against the system and start asking how the system should respond to them.

Jordan's label brought access, but it also narrowed the way people saw him. Every decision, every assumption, was filtered through that label. What he needed wasn't a clearer diagnosis. He needed someone to look past it.

Seeing the Label, Understanding the Person

Certain diagnoses come up more frequently than others. They are the ones you hear a lot: autism, ADHD, and dyslexia. They come up in meetings, on paper, and in the way people speak about students. Because they're well-known, people think they understand them. That's not always the case.

Autism: Spectrum or Continuum?

Autism is often described as a spectrum, but what that means to individual people varies. Some use it to describe a single sliding scale, from "mild" to "severe." Others think of it as a set of overlapping traits that look different from person to person. And both perspectives hold some truth.

Two students can have the same label and need very different things. One might talk constantly and still need sensory breaks to stay regulated. Another might barely speak but fly through complex puzzles. The label gives us a name, but it doesn't tell us what support looks like in practice.

Some educators like the term spectrum because it captures how different the traits can be across individuals. Others prefer continuum because it frames those traits as part of a broader range of human experience. Everyone struggles with social communication sometimes. Everyone has sensory preferences. Traits like sensitivity to noise or the need for routine don't only belong to autism.

Both terms get used, sometimes interchangeably, but they mean different things. Spectrum refers to the range of traits within autism. Continuum means those traits also show up in people without a diagnosis. Understanding the difference is significant. It changes how we talk about students and how we plan for their support.

Quick Metaphor

Spectrum is like a rainbow, showing different traits in different combinations.

A continuum is more like a dial. It doesn't sort people into categories, it shows where they fall along a shared range.

The Centers for Disease Control and Prevention (2025) reports that 1 in 31 children in the United States is now identified as being diagnosed with autism. But in many schools, public understanding hasn't caught up. The label continues to be collapsed into surface-level shorthand, as if it alone can account for how a student communicates, behaves, or learns. But not everyone with autism looks the same. The label needs to be treated as a starting point, not a conclusion.

ADHD: More Than Just Focus

ADHD is one of the most commonly diagnosed conditions in school-aged children, but it's also one of the most casually referenced. It often becomes a punchline or a placeholder. "That's just his ADHD" is a phrase you hear in schools as though the diagnosis explains everything. But ADHD is complex. It can affect attention, yes, but also working memory, emotional regulation, and executive function. Some students may struggle to sit still. Others may seem inattentive or disconnected. Many, especially girls, learn to mask their symptoms and end up underdiagnosed or misidentified.

The label "ADHD" should never be the end of the conversation. It should be the beginning of better questions. What kind of tasks are hard to start? When does focus improve? Are breaks helpful or frustrating? There are no universal strategies for everyone with an ADHD diagnosis. Not everyone needs the same things. What they need is the same curiosity and care we offer to any learner.

Dyslexia: Misunderstood but Common

Dyslexia is common. Some estimate up to one in five students (Wagner et al., 2020). The actual rate depends on how you define and measure it, but either way, it shows up in schools every day. And it's still widely misunderstood. Many people still think it's reversing letters or reading words upside down. Dyslexia isn't a result of seeing letters backward. That myth still creeps up, but it's always been beside the point.

What is actually happening is a mismatch between how a student processes print and how schools are accustomed to teaching reading. The majority of students with dyslexia have trouble decoding. They need to put in more effort to figure out the sounds behind the letters (Shaywitz, 2003). Fluency is another hurdle. Reading takes more time, more effort. And while that slows things down, it doesn't mean the student doesn't understand. In fact, many of them are strong thinkers. Some can explain things out loud with clarity far beyond their peers. Others are sharp with visuals or patterns. But when reading is slow, people often stop looking for what's working. The struggle takes up all the space.

Sometimes dyslexia gets missed for years. Especially when the student behaves well, tries hard, and finds ways to cope. In other cases, it gets brushed off as a motivation issue. The student is told they simply need to focus more or try harder. Then comes the pull-outs and the interventions. The messages, repeated over time, that they are behind. That they're not keeping up. Eventually, some students start to believe it.

Understanding a student's label is only part of the picture. We also have to look at how those labels are formed. Behind every diagnosis is a process. A process that is often complex and sometimes inconsistent.

Evaluations are supposed to bring clarity, and sometimes they do. However, other times, they miss what counts the most. We are what we ask, what tools we use, and how we read the results. Our reading of those results determines what comes next for the student, and if we're not mindful, we begin to make our decisions based on a diagnosis, rather than the learner sitting in front of us.

The Complexities of Special Education Evaluations

Special education evaluations are often seen as definitive. A clean, clinical process designed to measure a student's needs and determine the right path forward. Unfortunately, that's not the full story. Evaluations aren't simply diagnostic; they are very much human. They are influenced by the people administering them, the tools they chose, and the context in which they are working.

This isn't the equivalent of a medical test with a fixed result. Two evaluators could assess the same student and walk away with very different conclusions. This comes up a lot when schools are trying to identify a Specific Learning Disability (SLD). IDEA says students have to be evaluated, but it doesn't say how. The method isn't standardized. It's up to the state, the district, or sometimes even the individual team running the evaluation.

I was reminded of this during a professional conference on best practices for SLD identification. One participant confidently described his district's use of cross-battery assessment. Someone else pushed back, pointing out that the research base behind that method is weak. Another person chimed in to say their district uses the "pattern of strengths and weaknesses" approach, which was quickly critiqued for similar concerns. A third mentioned the discrepancy model. It used to be one of the more common methods, but that didn't hold up either. Plenty of states have moved away from it, and the concerns haven't gone away.

By the end of the conversation, we all arrived at the same uncomfortable truth: no method is universally accepted. Each has flaws. Each has supporters and skeptics. And all of them carry implications for who is identified, who is missed, and what kind of support follows.

The Influence of Bias in Testing

Cultural bias adds another layer of complexity to special education evaluations, especially in cognitive assessments. Standardized tests, including many IQ measures, have a long and troubling history. Many were developed in environments shaped by narrow assumptions that reflected dominant cultural values and ignored the diversity of student experiences (Helms, 1992). There have been attempts to mitigate bias, but it still persists in how these tests are constructed as well as how they are interpreted.

A student from a nondominant culture may struggle with questions rooted in unfamiliar customs or idioms. In those moments, it's not ability being measured, it's familiarity.

These details are worth our time. If an evaluation team doesn't fully consider how a student's background impacts their performance, the results can start to lose accuracy. One misunderstood score can lead to the wrong label. That label can change the way adults respond and even the way a student starts to see themselves.

When Labels Become Limits

Labels often carry more weight than intended. They are supposed to open doors to connect students with support, services, and people who understand their needs. However, they can just as easily close those same doors. For many students, a label becomes the first thing others see, and sometimes, the only thing they remember.

Once a student is labeled, expectations change. Teachers might lower the bar without realizing it. Peers might offer sympathy instead of inclusion. Over time, the student may begin to internalize those signals. What begins as support can start to feel like a ceiling.

This is even more important when we remember how uneven evaluations can be. If a student's strengths don't come through clearly in the data, or if the team overlooks something essential, the label that follows can miss who the student actually is. That label can then influence how adults plan. It can narrow which classes the student gets placed in, how much support is offered, and how much challenge is even considered.

I've watched students get pulled from art, science, or music. Classes where their disability wasn't even part of the equation.

Someone decided the task might be too hard. I've heard people say, "I don't want him to get upset," or "I don't think she can do this," before the student had a chance to try. Those decisions weren't usually made with bad intent. They came from concern. But when concern leads to lowered expectations, school stops being a place where students get to figure things out.

The system asks us to get through a lot: documents, timelines, and decisions. It's easy to fall into patterns. Teams look for eligibility, skim the scores, and flip to the recommendations. That's not negligence, but it too often is a habit. When we stop paying attention to what's not written down, we miss chances to understand the student more fully. What do these results actually show about how this student learns? What do they leave out? Where can we look again?

We need to treat the evaluation as a starting point, not the end point. When we proceed with it that way, we leave more room for students to show us who they are. We make space for potential to surprise us. We remind ourselves that every label, every score, every summary should lead us closer to understanding the student, not narrowing who they're allowed to become.

The Role of IDEA and Safeguards

To its credit, IDEA includes important safeguards intended to prevent mislabeling and bias. One such safeguard is the requirement that evaluations be conducted by a multidisciplinary team. This approach brings teachers, specialists, and school psychologists together so that no one perspective drives the whole decision. The point is to look at the student from more than one angle, hoping pieces don't get missed.

Another protection under IDEA is the right to request an Independent Educational Evaluation (IEE). If families disagree with the school's findings, they can request that a separate, qualified professional conduct a new evaluation. The district is responsible for covering the cost, making it another option in special education that does not come with a financial burden for parents. In theory, this creates a powerful check on the system.

One that helps prevent misidentification, confirm findings, or bring in a new perspective.

And it can absolutely do that.

The IEE can be misapplied, sometimes requested out of frustration rather than a true problem with the evaluation. That doesn't mean families shouldn't use it, but the conditions around it are meaningful. Families don't usually ask for an IEE when things are going well. Maybe a concern was dismissed. Maybe the explanation didn't make sense. Somewhere along the way, the family likely felt like they weren't listened to. For many families, the IEE is seen as a last resort or a necessary safeguard against the school.

An IEE can still be part of that partnership. One where disagreement is respected, but not assumed to be adversarial. One where both sides stay focused on what is the most important: understanding the student. Safeguards like the IEE exist for a reason. Evaluations don't always get it right the first time. Sometimes teams miss things, and families notice what others don't. That second opinion holds value, whether we like it or not. These protections work best when the home-school connection is strong. One where there's honest dialog, space to ask questions, and a common goal of getting it right for the student, which goes beyond process.

Moving to a More Holistic Approach

A better evaluation process starts with how we think about students. We cannot think of our students as profiles, nor as scores. We have to think of them as learners with real lives and histories that don't always show up on a form.

Context and a student's background have a place. Everything from the language a child speaks, to the culture they belong to, and even what's going on at home can affect how they engage in school and react to testing. When we leave that out, we risk getting the data wrong. A low score doesn't always mean low skill. Sometimes it means the questions weren't designed for how that student thinks or communicates. Good evaluators ask more than "What did the student get wrong?" They ask, "What else could explain this result?" and "What are we not seeing yet?"

Evaluator self-awareness is important too. Bias doesn't always show up in obvious ways. It can show up in small decisions. How we frame a question. What we assume about behavior. Which patterns we notice and which we ignore. Taking time to examine our own lens is part of the process. We can't talk about accuracy without talking about how our perspective shapes what we see.

A strong evaluation pulls from more than one source. Of course, standardized data is part of the whole picture, but so are classroom observations, work samples, interviews, and, where possible, the student's voice. Families know what motivates or shuts down their child, and that perspective is essential. These pieces do more than simply confirm eligibility; they allow us to understand how student learning is occurring and what supports will actually be meaningful.

Done well, an evaluation gives direction. It shows where support is needed, where something is already working, and where the student might surprise us if we knew how to look.

Moving Forward: Recognizing Strengths Beyond the Label

Far too often, these challenging behaviors are viewed as problems to be managed and not as signs of unmet needs or latent strengths. Jordan was always "the problem student" on virtually any campus he was on. His silent nature and history of behavior problems made it easy for teachers to concentrate on what was hard about his behavior and fail to see what his problems were beneath the surface. When one school, at last, took a closer look, they saw something else.

Turnbull et al. (2006) describe how IDEA's framework, while designed to support individualized education, can sometimes lead to restrictive patterns. Labels meant to guide support can overshadow the full potential of the student behind them. Jordan's experience is not unique. When systems rely too heavily on what's documented in a file, they risk missing the deeper strengths that aren't as easily measured.

I was reminded of this again at a conference presentation on inclusive practices. The presenters shared a short video featuring a young girl, maybe six or seven years old, in a rural district that clearly wasn't flush with resources. She had a one-on-one aide to assist with safety and self-care, but she was a full participant in the general education classroom. Her classmates knew when to remind her to line up, when to help redirect her gently, and when to simply let her be. I don't even remember her diagnosis. Maybe that's the point. What I remember most was the natural way her peers supported her. They weren't trained to do this. They were merely given permission to treat her like she belonged.

These are the stories that help us remember what can happen when we stop and take the time to notice what we might otherwise miss. This is what can happen when we really look. They teach us that every student has something to offer, even if it's not easily visible.

Recognizing strengths beyond the label isn't an extra. We have to think about that as part of how we plan, how we support, how we create a schoolwide culture where every student feels like they are seen as individuals. When we start with belief, when we assume that there is more to know, we start to construct something more responsive.

Recognizing strengths is only part of the work. We also have to examine the patterns and habits within our systems that can unintentionally hold students back. The ways we talk about support, the labels we rely on, and the structures we follow all shape the student experience. And sometimes, without meaning to, those practices create more distance than connection.

Critiquing Common Practices: Moving Toward Individualized Understanding

Labels still drive too many decisions. In some schools, students with an autism label are pulled from general education as a first step, based on the assumption that they won't be able to manage typical instruction. Jorgensen and Lambert (2012) found that students with autism and other developmental disabilities were often physically present in general education settings, but not meaningfully included. Too many were taught mostly by paraprofessionals, seated apart from peers, and left without access to the curriculum. Those patterns came from assumptions about the label, not student need, and unchallenged assumptions limit opportunities.

The same thing happens with emotional disability. A label meant to provide access to resources and support starts to act more like a warning. That's what happened with Jordan. Before he ever spoke, teams had already formed an idea of who he was and what he would bring. It became harder to see anything beyond the file.

Labels can help when they guide support. The risk is when they start doing all the talking. If no one asks better questions, the label becomes the whole story. And when that story stays unchallenged, students lose chances to be seen differently.

Getting this right doesn't mean we throw labels out. It means we use them differently. As a way in, not a final word. Real understanding comes from time, connection, and attention to the full student, not only what's written in the paperwork.

Practical Strategies: Unmasking the Individual in Every Student

Seeing students for who they are, not only how they're labeled, takes intentional work. It means building in moments to notice, listen, and connect. And it means putting tools in place that help us get past assumptions and into the details that really tell us what is important. Here are a few strategies that can help bring that into everyday practice:

> **Interest Inventories**: One practical way to learn about a student beyond what's written in their file is to ask what they like. What they do outside of school. What they care about. Interest inventories can be a set of short questions, a

warm-up routine, or a one-on-one conversation. You don't need to worry about getting every question right. What is essential is giving students a chance to be known for something other than a diagnosis.

That kind of information helps. Especially when a student is hard to reach. It gives us a place to start. A small way in. With Jordan, a teacher mentioned a musician he liked, and he responded. It was the first time he'd spoken more than a sentence in days. That helped him feel seen and started building trust.

Brenna et al. (2017) found that even simple interest inventories helped future teachers make stronger connections with students and shape more relevant instruction. It didn't take a complicated system. It took asking questions, listening, and using what students shared to guide the next steps.

Asset Mapping: When teams talk about what a student needs, the conversation often starts with what's missing. Asset mapping flips that. It asks, "What's already working?" and "What does this student bring?" That could mean skills, interests, family and community connections, or strategies that help the student feel safe and capable.

Morgan et al. (2022) describe asset mapping as a way to shift focus, especially for students with emotional or behavioral needs. Instead of tracking deficits, teams work together to name what supports the student and where they already succeed. That information can change how we plan.

When we build from strengths, students are more likely to see themselves as part of the classroom, not outside of it. And teachers are more likely to create support plans that last because they're based on something the student already knows how to do.

Reflective Practice for Educators: The concern for students does not remove bias from the equation. Even the most accomplished teachers fall into patterns like making up their minds too fast about what a student can or can't do, responding to behavior without stopping to wonder what's really driving it, lowering expectations without even being fully aware they're doing it. It's why regular reflection can be important. It encourages us to recognize repetitive events that we might otherwise miss during a full day.

It doesn't have to be formal. Sometimes it's as simple as asking, "What have I actually seen this student do?" or "Am I responding to the student in front of me, or to the label in their file?" Questions like these pull our attention back to what is most important.

Reflection helps us pay attention and gives us a chance to adjust. It's what lets us course-correct in real time. How we see a student affects the decisions we make. It can shape the opportunities they get, or the ones they never have a chance to try.

Building Relationships through Curiosity: Sometimes the most important strategy is simply staying curious. When we stop assuming and start asking, we get better information. A student who refuses group work might not be avoiding the task. They might not know how to join in or what's expected in that setting. Paying attention to those moments helps us respond with more clarity and less assumption.

These tools aren't a fix. They're a way to get better information and build real connection, especially when the paperwork doesn't tell us enough. When used regularly, they help us see more of the student than what's written in a file. They make opportunities for students to be known in ways that actually are significant.

Lloyd Dunn (1968) pushed back on the idea that students with disabilities should be taught in separate settings. His work reminds us that real inclusion isn't only about where students are placed. It's about how they are understood. And that starts when we look for strengths, build relationships, and create systems that actually respond to students as they are.

Beyond Labels: Seeing the Whole Student

Seeing the whole student means looking beyond academic performance alone. Some students shut down during math but open up during art. Others fall behind during group work but stay focused when given time to work on their own. Those differences matter. They tell us when a student is overwhelmed, when they're engaged, and when something is finally clicking. We miss all of that if we only focus on what's hard.

Labels can help teams start planning, but they leave a lot out. If we want to understand students, we have to stay with what's real. What we see. What they show us in the small moments, not just what's typed in a plan.

A Call to Action: Unmasking Potential in Every Student

The role of education isn't to simply manage learning. It's to meet each student as they are and help them move forward. That work begins when we look past the shorthand of eligibility categories and ask better questions. Who is this student? What holds most value to them? What strengths haven't we seen yet?

Each student's story is still unfolding. When we lead with curiosity and build support that fits the learner, we create something better. Special education isn't about fixing students. It's about seeing their potential clearly enough not to miss it.

References

Algozzine, B., Ysseldyke, J. E., & Christenson, S. (1977). The influence of labels on special education students' self-concepts. *Journal of Special Education, 11*(3), 339–347.

Brenna, B., Myburgh, J.-E., Aubichon, S., Baker, A., Fee, R., Hounsell, S., Kennedy, L., Kennedy, S., Pilon, J., & Thomas, S. (2017). Exploring the use of interest inventories with elementary students: A rich foundation for literacy curriculum making. *The Reading Professor, 39*(1), Article 6. https://scholar.stjohns.edu/thereadingprofessor/vol39/iss1/6

Centers for Disease Control and Prevention. (2025). Data & statistics on autism spectrum disorder. https://www.cdc.gov/autism/data-research/index.html

Dunn, L. M. (1968). Special education for the mildly retarded—is much of it justifiable? *Exceptional Children, 35*(1), 5–22.

Goffman, E. (1963). *Stigma: Notes on the management of spoiled identity.* Prentice-Hall.

Helms, J. E. (1992). Why is there no study of cultural equivalence in standardized cognitive ability testing? *American Psychologist, 47*(9), 1083–1101.

Individuals with Disabilities Education Act, 20 U.S.C. § 1400 (2004).

Jorgensen, C. M., & Lambert, L. (2012). Inclusion means more than just being "in": Planning full participation of students with intellectual and other developmental disabilities in the general education classroom. *International Journal of Whole Schooling, 8*(2), 21–36.

Morgan, J. J., Bengochea, A., & Reed, J. (2022). Asset mapping in urban environments to support students with emotional and behavioral disorders. *Intervention in School and Clinic, 58*(2), 100–109. https://doi.org/10.1177/10534512211051072

Rosenthal, R., & Jacobson, L. (1968). *Pygmalion in the classroom: Teacher expectation and pupils' intellectual development.* Holt, Rinehart & Winston.

Shaywitz, S. E. (2003). *Overcoming dyslexia: A new and complete science-based program for reading problems at any level.* Alfred A. Knopf.

Skrtic, T. M. (1991). *Behind special education: A critical analysis of professional culture and school organization.* Love Publishing Company.

Turnbull, H. R., Stowe, M., & Huerta, N. E. (2006). *Free appropriate public education: The law and children with disabilities* (7th ed.). Love Publishing Company.

Wagner, R. K., Zirps, F. A., Edwards, A. A., Wood, S. G., Joyner, R. E., Becker, B. J., Liu, G., & Beal, B. (2020). The prevalence of dyslexia: A new approach to its estimation. *Journal of Learning Disabilities, 53*(5), 354–365. https://doi.org/10.1177/0022219420920377

3

Sidekicks in the Classroom
Inclusion and Technology

Depending on when you went to school, classroom technology might bring up different memories: like floppy disks and *Oregon Trail*, a TV strapped to a rolling cart with a teacher fumbling with the VCR or scribbled transparency notes under the humming glow of an overhead projector. Either way, most of us, of a certain age, didn't grow up with the kind of technology that's available to students today.

Now, it's everywhere. The tools at our disposal would have been well beyond our wildest dreams even a decade ago. Things like speech-to-text, immersive reading apps, digital portfolios, and even artificial intelligence (AI) that can spit out a study guide in seconds. But here's what isn't different: the tools were never really the point. It's about what we do with them.

Technology can fall apart fast. Just when you've figured something out, it updates or disappears. I once worked with a team that swore by this brilliant little app to track student behavior and send daily reports home. It was simple, effective, and parents actually read the updates. Then one day, we got a notice: the app was being discontinued at the end of the month. There was no replacement and nothing lined up to take its place. It was simply gone.

We scrambled to replace it, but nothing was as good. I didn't think too much of it at the time, but that moment changed how I thought about suggesting specific technology. These days, I rarely suggest a specific app. Instead, I look at what it needs to accomplish, so if one program disappears, there's still a path forward. Novak and Woodlock (2021) say the same thing in their *UDL Playbook*, reminding leaders to plan for the function, not the brand name. Whether it's reducing barriers and creating flexible options that support executive function. When the goal is clear, teams can adapt, even when the tools change.

These days, when we talk about technology in schools, we're also talking about AI.

AI is not on the horizon. It's already here. When ChatGPT launched in late 2022, over a million people signed up in five days (Curran et al., 2024). For context, it took Facebook ten months to reach that milestone. Instagram needed two and a half months. Netflix took more than three and a half years. ChatGPT's speed wasn't only about novelty; it was about utility. People, especially educators, were trying to figure out what this could mean for learning. Some were excited, others were nervous, while many were both. All of them were asking some version of the same question: what do we do with this?

That's the thing about AI. It doesn't wait around for us to catch up. It evolves faster than most educational systems can respond. But pretending it doesn't exist, or hoping it goes away, isn't going to work. The more helpful question isn't "Should we use it?" but "How can we use it well?"

Especially in special education, where the need for differentiation, access, and flexibility is part of the everyday work. AI has potential here. AI can help teachers by handling some routine tasks, giving them more time to focus on thoughtful connections and stronger inclusion practices.

But thoughtful doesn't have to mean overwhelming. You don't have to be a tech wizard to start integrating AI or other tools into your practice. In fact, it helps to think about technology use in levels, not as a rigid ladder, but more like stages of comfort and curiosity (Table 3.1).

Wherever you land on that scale, the focus should stay on students, because when technology is applied with intention, it can help remove obstacles and expand connections by amplifying student voice.

TABLE 3.1 Levels of AI Integration in Inclusive Classrooms

Stage	What It Looks Like	Questions to Ask
AI Explorer	You're testing out a few basic tools. Maybe a speech-to-text feature, some translations, or a chatbot for quick writing prompts. Focus stays on noticing: what works, what doesn't, and how it fits student learning.	What does this tool actually help with? Where does it fall short? Is it supporting student learning?
Integration Champion	You've found tools that genuinely make things easier. Maybe you're adapting texts faster or building visual supports with less hassle. You're not using tech for tech's sake, but to respond to student needs, and you might even be sharing ideas with colleagues.	How is this improving instruction? Are students more engaged or independent? What could be refined?
Innovator and Co-creator	You've moved beyond simply using tools. You're giving feedback to developers, co-designing with students, or shaping the tech approach for your school. You're thinking system-wide, not just classroom-level.	How can this tool evolve? What do students say they want? How does this support equity and inclusion?

A student with dyslexia puts on headphones and listens to a version of the text that's been adjusted, not watered down, but actually made readable. The story is still there, and the language finally makes sense. Across the room, another student is talking into a Chromebook. They're trying to get their thoughts out before they disappear. Later, they'll sit with a partner and clean it up together. Off to the side, a third kid is asking a chatbot for metaphors about dinosaurs, because that's what they're into right now, and they're planning to build a whole piece around it. Meanwhile, the teacher is up, moving, checking in. They are not stuck behind a desk editing passages or redrawing visual schedules, but actually getting to teach. When tools like text-to-speech, translation support, or visual planning apps are integrated into general instruction, they expand student access and support more independent participation across learning settings (Al-Azawei et al., 2016).

That's not some future dream. It's happening in real classrooms where AI helps remove barriers and open up access.

Educators are using AI in real, practical ways. They're:

- Drafting behavior plans tailored to a student's context.
- Generating social stories based on real-life routines.
- Building visual schedules, token boards, and choice menus in seconds instead of hours.
- Translating classroom updates into plain language across multiple home languages.
- Creating options for how students show what they know: a podcast script, a slide deck outline, or even a solid sentence starter for someone who needs a little push.
- Getting unstuck while lesson planning by asking for ideas that line up with a student's Individual Educational Programs (IEPs) goals and keep the work meaningful.

Often when we think about AI in the classrooms, we imagine these high-tech labs. This isn't that. It's about helping educators get back to the part of the job that counts the most, which is connecting with students.

Of course, the tools aren't perfect. AI can hallucinate, reinforce bias, or spit out something totally off-base (Al-Zahrani, 2024). That's why it needs you. Not only to supervise, but to think critically. To test, adjust, and decide when something is worth using and when it's not. At its best, AI isn't replacing professional judgment. It's helping you move faster toward the parts of your job that actually require it.

Some of the most effective uses aren't fancy, they're frankly smart:

- A school psychologist drafting a plain-language summary for a parent who's overwhelmed.
- A paraeducator printing a quick-read story tied to a student's specific interest so they'll actually read it.
- A teacher making three versions of a math word problem: one about food, one about football, and one about Minecraft, so every group has an entry point.

And we're still barely getting started.

Want to support executive functioning? Co-create checklists and planners with your students.

What about helping students reflect on their needs? Let them co-write self-reflection prompts.

Building conflict resolution skills? Use AI to model different choices and outcomes before the moment happens in real life.

How about pushing your own thinking? Ask AI to play devil's advocate and to challenge your assumptions – to help reframe a student behavior in language that's more accurate and less deficit-driven.

None of this means throwing out research-based practices. It means extending them and reframing the question from "How will I get all of this done?" to "What might help me do it better?" That's the real promise: not speed for its own sake, but a way to work smarter. With more intention, and in ways that feel more human.

Still, for many, the mention of "technology" often lands with a thud in educator conversations. For some, it brings excitement; for others, exhaustion. Especially when it's paired with AI, which can sound like one more thing to figure out in an already overstuffed day. That's a fair reaction. Try this instead: think of technology as a sidekick, not the star of the show, but a tool that helps the superhero (remember, that's you) do the work better.

This chapter explores how inclusion, co-teaching, and technology can intersect to create classrooms where all students, not just some, have a shot at meaningful participation. That means more than showing up. It means having real access, receiving steady support, and feeling a genuine sense of belonging.

Let's figure out how to get there.

Technology Meets Design: UDL Can Still Make a Difference

For all the buzz around AI and educational tech, the heart of an inclusive classroom still comes down to intentional design. Planning for the students in front of us comes first, before any discussion of tools. We also need to remember the ones who aren't quite ready to speak up yet.

That's where Universal Design for Learning (UDL) comes in.

UDL isn't new. The framework's been around since 2008, developed by CAST, and grounded in the idea that no two learners are exactly alike, so instruction shouldn't be either. At its core, UDL is a flexible approach to teaching that helps ensure all students can access learning in ways that work for them.

The updated UDL Guidelines 3.0, released in 2024, take things a step further (CAST, 2024). While earlier versions emphasized access and representation, the newest version pushes deeper into identity, community, and system-level change. It moves the focus away from simply "how do I present content in different ways?" to bigger questions: who gets to participate? Whose voice is centered? Who feels like they belong here?

UDL is built around three big ideas:

- **Engagement**: How do we spark interest and build motivation?
- **Representation**: How do we offer information in ways that make sense to different learners?
- **Action and Expression**: How do we give students flexible ways to show what they know?

And here's where technology becomes more than a set of tools. When used with care, it supports all three areas. It offers choice, removes barriers, and opens doors.

Take engagement. A student who struggles with traditional reading might light up when given access to immersive audio or visual storytelling. Or representation: a math concept that felt abstract on paper can become clearer through an interactive simulation. Action and expression? Students can create podcasts, visual essays, or voice recordings instead of writing out another five-paragraph response.

UDL doesn't mean "every student gets their own personalized plan." It means we build flexibility into the structure from the start. Instead of waiting for a student to struggle and then adjusting, we assume variability is the norm and design with that in mind.

And here's the part that can sometimes be misunderstood: UDL isn't about lowering expectations. It's about finding more ways for students to meet them. Technology can help with that, but only when we start with a clear purpose and let the tools follow, not the other way around.

Engagement: More Than Participation

The first principle of UDL is engagement, but don't confuse that with just keeping students busy. Engagement happens through connection, not gimmicks. It's about helping students care, giving them a reason to be present, and making certain they see themselves in the learning.

That can be tough when the schedule is tight, the pacing guide is unyielding, and half the class is still behind from last week. But it's not impossible.

Technology used thoughtfully can help us open up support and structure for voice, identity, and choice. Three things that we often leave out when we talk about student engagement. When students with disabilities, English learners, or students who've been historically marginalized see themselves reflected in the work, they're far more likely to show up with curiosity instead of resistance.

Let's take digital choice boards. Instead of assigning the same activity to every student, you give them options. Some might record a podcast reflection, others could draw a comic strip, or stick with a traditional written response. Same content, different paths in. Tools like Canva, Book Creator, or even the built-in video recorder on a Chromebook can make that possible without adding extra work for the teacher.

Gamified platforms can work too, not because they're fun (though that helps), but because they allow students to get feedback in real time. Programs like Prodigy, Legends of Learning, or Blooket offer more than digital noise. Used intentionally, they help students feel a sense of growth and momentum. Research backs this up. In a study with middle school students with learning disabilities, Marino et al. (2014) found that when video games and text were used alongside traditional content, students showed higher levels of engagement. The UDL-aligned approach of offering multiple ways to access material and show what they know helped students stay connected and involved.

But engagement isn't really about tools. It's about whether students feel like they belong in the place to begin with. One teacher I worked with created a weekly "Student Spotlight" where learners got to showcase something important to them. This could be a photo, a family recipe, or a favorite memory. It wasn't fancy. A simple Google Slides deck and five minutes on Friday. But it changed the way students saw each other, and the way they showed up for learning.

UDL 3.0 leans heavily into this idea of belonging. It asks us to think not only about how we motivate students, but how we build a classroom that feels emotionally safe, culturally responsive, and genuinely connected to who students are.

If you are wondering where to begin with UDL or with educational tech, period, start here. Not with a new app, but with this question: does every student feel like this classroom is meant for them?

Because when students feel seen, they're far more likely to engage. And when they engage, learning follows.

Representation: More Than One Way to See It

Not all students learn the same way. That's not a new idea, but most curriculum materials still act like it is. We see it in the text-heavy slides, the single textbook, the one "right" answer waiting at the end of the chapter.

The UDL principle of representation challenges that. It challenges us to reconsider how we deliver information so that all students, no matter their backgrounds, language skills, learning profiles, or disabilities, can actually understand what is being taught.

Technology can help with this. Not because it replaces good instruction, but because it gives us options. Offering students choices in how they access content and show what they know impacts how connected they feel. Fleming (2023) found that when classrooms use tools like digital choice boards and media formats within a UDL framework, students reported higher levels of engagement and a stronger sense of belonging.

Say you are teaching a new concept in science. A more traditional approach might consist of a brief lecture and some vocabulary words written on the board. But a more flexible iteration could be a short video (with closed captions), a diagram students can manipulate on a touchscreen, or a shared slide deck with terms in multiple languages. Students are still receiving the same content with more ways in.

For a student with processing delays or reading challenges, something as simple as turning on closed captions or using a tool like Immersive Reader can make a big difference. For English learners, visual supports, translations, or voice-overs can help connect what they already know to what they're being asked to learn.

And for all students, not only those with IEPs, graphic organizers, concept maps, and digital annotation tools like Kami or even the built-in markup tools in Google Docs can give structure without removing independence.

But representation isn't only about format. It's also about perspective. Who is telling the story? Whose knowledge counts? Who's included, and who's missing?

UDL 3.0 pushes this conversation further. It doesn't only ask how students receive content. It asks whether that content affirms who they are. A reading passage that includes names and stories familiar to your students does more than improve comprehension. It sends a signal: you belong here.

That's also where technology can help widen access. Online archives, global libraries, and open educational resources offer ways to expand beyond the textbook and include voices that are too often left out.

When students see themselves, and others, reflected in what they're learning, understanding deepens. So does trust. So does interest. For students who've spent years being overlooked or left out, that kind of recognition is important. Representation isn't only about access. It's about inclusion. Not, "Did the student hear the lesson?" but, "Did they see themselves in it?"

Action and Expression: Let Them Show You

If you've worked in classrooms for more than five minutes, you know that how students show what they've learned can look very different. One student might light up during class discussions but freeze during written assessments. Another might ace a hands-on project but shut down when faced with a timed test. And that's not an issue with effort. It's about access.

The third principle of UDL is action and expression. This is about providing students with options to demonstrate what they know. It recognizes that traditional assessments often reflect how a student communicates more than what they actually understand.

Technology gives us more ways to fix that.

One student struggles with writing but has a lot to say. When they're allowed to speak their thoughts out loud, the ideas come through. This could be a video reflection, a voice memo, or even speech-to-text. The thinking is there; it's the format that needs to be modified.

Another student has been working on a project for weeks. They've done the reading, taken notes, but asking them to write a timed essay doesn't show what they've learned. However, building a digital model or laying out a timeline might. Their knowledge doesn't disappear; it just needs a different way out.

Assistive technology helps make that possible. A student with motor challenges might use a touchscreen or an adapted keyboard to finish a task on their own. A student with language delays might lean on visual tools or sentence frames to get started. Think of these not as shortcuts, but as openings. And the beauty is, these supports often benefit students without IEPs too.

One middle school teacher I worked with gave her class a choice for every major assignment. Students could write, record, present, or design. At first, she worried it might lower expectations. What she saw instead was an increase in quality, effort, and ownership. Students picked the format that matched how they processed information. And when that match was right, their work spoke volumes. That mirrors what Anderson (2022) found in a book study lesson designed for students with intellectual disabilities. By planning with UDL from the start, the teacher gave students multiple ways to engage with the text and show their understanding. The results weren't about lowering the bar. They were about opening access.

Offering multiple means of expression doesn't mean watering things down. It means recognizing that students are more likely to show what they know when they're not limited by a single format.

In a classroom designed with UDL in mind, action and expression aren't an afterthought. They're part of the plan from the start. And when technology is used to open up those pathways, not to simplify the task but to give students a real way to show what they know, everyone benefits.

From Design to Delivery: Why Co-Teaching Still Has a Place

Designing a classroom with flexibility in mind is powerful. But even the most thoughtful lessons fall flat without the right support behind them. That's where co-teaching is especially impactful. If UDL helps us plan for learner variability, co-teaching helps us respond to it in real time.

This isn't as simple as having two adults in the same room. When done well, co-teaching brings together the knowledge of general and special educators in a way that benefits all students. The focus isn't on who's leading the lesson. What is worth noticing is what students need and how both teachers can work together to make that happen. Too often, co-teaching gets boiled down to one teacher leading while the other floats in the back. That's not collaboration, it's a missed opportunity.

Researchers have identified six common models of co-teaching (Zamkowska et al., 2025). Not all of them fit every lesson, but knowing them gives teams more ways to support access and engagement, especially when technology is part of the planning.

1. **One Teach, One Assist**
   One teacher leads the lesson. The other provides support to students as they work.

Example: While the lead teacher explains a reading strategy, the co-teacher moves around with a tablet and headphones, helping students follow the text with text-to-speech tools.

2. **One Teach, One Observe**
   One teacher leads while the other gathers information (e.g., who's engaged, who's confused, and who's not participating).
   Example: The observing teacher uses a checklist to track patterns and shares observations during planning.

3. **Station Teaching**
   Students rotate through stations. Some are teacher-led. Some are independent.
   Example: One station runs a science simulation. Another reviews content through a video and quiz. The third uses manipulatives or hands-on materials.

4. **Parallel Teaching**
   The class is split in half. Both teachers cover the same material in smaller groups.
   Example: One group uses manipulatives to solve math problems. The other works on the same skill using touchscreen tools.

5. **Alternative Teaching**
   One teacher works with most of the class. The other leads a small group for targeted instruction.
   Example: A few students use speech-to-text tools to revise a draft with one teacher, while the rest work on peer editing with the other.

6. **Team Teaching**
   Both teachers share responsibility for the full group. They lead, respond, and adjust together.
   Example: During a class discussion, one teacher facilitates while the other models note-taking or runs a quick check-in poll on student devices.

Each model has a purpose. But relying on only one can limit what's possible (Zamkowska et al., 2025). Some models work better than others, depending on the goal. Maybe the aim is to lower stress, get more students talking, or give someone a win who hasn't had one in a while. Technology can help with that, but only if both teachers are engaged and students know how it's going to work.

The model itself isn't what makes the difference. What cannot be ignored is whether students can actually get into the learning. When co-teaching is part of the plan from the start, it stops being a workaround and starts being real support.

Wrapping the Threads: Matching Tools to Needs

At this stage, it might feel like the list of strategies, tools, and models could go on forever. And honestly, it probably could. But trying to do it all isn't the move. The goal is about making choices that actually make sense for your students.

Technology alone doesn't guarantee better learning. Co-teaching doesn't guarantee inclusion. UDL only works when connected to real student needs. Instead of questioning what's new or what's in, it should be: "What's the problem I'm trying to address?"

For a student who has difficulty ordering their thoughts, you might try a visual planning tool. If a student doesn't want to speak in front of the class, perhaps they submit a video reflection or post on a shared Padlet. A student is overwhelmed by lengthy texts? Perhaps he or she can connect to that content through listening, images, and discussion in a small group.

The focus is on choosing tools that actually support the students in front of you, not merely collecting whatever's new.

Reflection: Inclusion Is a Practice, Not a Feature

Inclusion isn't something we tack on once everything else is done. It's not the thing we do for a few students. It's the way we design, plan, teach, and respond every day.

Technology can help, as can co-teaching, but only if we remember the actual goal: belonging, participation, opportunity, and real access. The truth is, when classrooms are planned with that kind of intention, they don't just work better for students with IEPs. They work better for everyone.

That's what it all comes down to: the planning, the tools, and the partnership. Every student should have a real place in the classroom. One where they can show up, take part, and be taken seriously.

References

Al-Azawei, A., Serenelli, F., & Lundqvist, K. (2016). Universal design for learning (UDL): A content analysis of peer-reviewed journal papers from 2012 to 2015. *Journal of the Scholarship of Teaching and Learning*, *16*(3), 39–56. https://doi.org/10.14434/josotl.v16i3.19295

Al-Zahrani, A. M. (2024). Unveiling the shadows: Beyond the hype of AI in education. *Heliyon*, *10*(9), e30696. https://doi.org/10.1016/j.heliyon.2024.e30696

Anderson, L. K. (2022). Using UDL to plan a book study lesson for students with intellectual disabilities in inclusive classrooms. *Teaching Exceptional Children*, *54*(4), 258–267. https://doi.org/10.1177/00400599211010196

CAST. (2024). *Universal Design for Learning guidelines version 3.0*. https://udlguidelines.cast.org

Curran, K., Curran, E., Killen, J., & Duffy, C. (2024). The role of generative AI in cyber security. *Metaverse*, *5*(2), 2796. https://doi.org/10.54517/m2796

Fleming, E. C. (2023). UDL for inclusive teaching: Offering choice to increase belonging through technology [Special issue]. *Journal of Teaching and Learning with Technology*, *12*, 72–90. https://doi.org/10.14434/jotlt.v12i1.36327

Marino, M. T., Gotch, C. M., Israel, M., Vasquez, E., Basham, J. D., & Becht, K. (2014). UDL in the middle school science classroom: Can video games and alternative text heighten engagement and learning for students with learning disabilities. *Learning Disability Quarterly*, *37*(2), 87–99. https://doi.org/10.1177/0731948713503963

Novak, K., & Woodlock, M. (2021). *UDL playbook for school and district leaders (UDL now!)*. CAST Professional Publishing.

Zamkowska, A., Pilgrim, M., & Hornby, G. (2025). Co-teaching: Review and guidelines for practice. *Preventing School Failure: Alternative Education for Children and Youth, 69*(2), 111–117. https://doi.org/10.1080/1045988X.2024.2404404

4

Redefining the Fortress of Solitude

Embracing Inclusive Environments

Remember Destiny from the beginning of this book? On paper, she was in the least restrictive environment (LRE): a general education classroom and supported by a paraeducator. It all looked compliant, technically inclusive.

Before we revisit her experience, let's talk about what LRE actually means. Under the Individuals with Disabilities Education Act (IDEA), the LRE requirement says that students with disabilities should be educated with their nondisabled peers to the *maximum extent appropriate*. They should only be removed from general education settings when, even with the use of supplementary aids and services, they can't be successfully supported in that environment.

That's the technical, legal version, but not especially helpful in practice. If you're a parent, a teacher, or anyone trying to make sense of what this looks like day to day, that kind of definition might still leave you guessing.

So here's a more straightforward explanation: LRE is supposed to make sure kids with disabilities aren't unnecessarily separated from everyone else. It's about giving them access to learning, friendships, and the full life of school. We're not talking about compliance for the sake of compliance. It's about asking, "Is this where this child can learn and connect best, with the right support?"

Now here's the part that often gets lost: that answer won't look the same for every student. It changes depending on what a child needs, and when. For some students, that might mean being in the general education classroom full-time with minimal supports. For others, it might involve spending part of the day in a smaller setting where they can focus, regroup, or receive targeted instruction. Inclusion is more than where a student sits. It asks whether students can connect, participate, and learn.

Now, this is where things start to blur.

Labels Don't Equal Connection

We tend to treat LRE and inclusion like synonyms. We throw around both terms as if they mean the same thing. In most states, LRE is measured by how much time a student spends in the general education classroom. There are even specific categories: students who are in general education 80% or more of the time, students who are there less than 40%, and so on. States track these numbers. Districts compare their percentages. It fits the compliance metrics, but not much else.

None of that tells you whether the child feels like part of the class.

Let's go back to Destiny. Her paperwork said she was in her LRE. She spent more than 80% of her school day in the general education classroom. That alone might lead someone to say she was "included."

But she wasn't, not really.

While her peers worked together at their tables, Destiny sat off to the side with her instructional assistant. When the teacher asked a question, she didn't raise her hand. She turned to her aide. When there was group work, she wasn't part of a group. Her assignments were different, her partner was an adult, and her role in the room was separate.

The Power of Intentional Support

The issue isn't paraeducators themselves, as many are lifelines. They're underpaid, undertrained, and asked to do demanding work without clear direction. Too often, paraeducators are dropped into classrooms without a clear plan. They're expected to support the student but often aren't told how. Sometimes they don't even know what the student is working on, let alone have access to the IEP or a seat at the planning table. In that kind of vacuum, even well-meaning help can turn into over-helping. When that happens, the student ends up tethered to the adult instead of forming real connections in the classroom.

The solution isn't to remove the support, it's to design it better. Paraeducators need real training, not only on compliance, but on how to fade support, how to prompt without prompting over, and how to scaffold interaction instead of replacing it. Equally important, they need to be part of the team. That means time to collaborate with teachers, chances to ask questions, and trust that their insight is important. What if we stopped asking paraeducators to do everything and started preparing them to do the right things well?

When paraeducators are supported well, they're not only helping students, they're helping build belonging.

Destiny's story forces us to ask better questions. The better questions sound more like this (Table 4.1).

If we're going to say "inclusion," it has to reflect real engagement, not just a shared place.

TABLE 4.1 Questions to Consider When Looking Beyond Academic Inclusion

Area	Questions to Ask
Social Connections	Who does she eat lunch with? Who are her friends?
Participation	Does she join group activities, or does she stay on the outside looking in?
Belonging	Has she ever been invited to a birthday party or other social event?

Belonging Isn't on the IEP

Here's the uncomfortable truth: it's entirely possible for a student to meet the legal definition of LRE and still be completely excluded from the life of the classroom. The law helps protect access, but it doesn't guarantee belonging. And that's where we, as educators, families, and schools, have to do the heavier lifting.

When we focus only on placement, minutes, and data points, we risk missing what is most meaningful. What does it mean to be part of something real? Who notices when someone's missing? Inclusion isn't about where you are. It's about how the environment works, and whether it welcomes everyone. A daily effort to make sure every child feels noticed, valued, and part of the group. For kids like Destiny, that difference is more impactful than most people realize. Location plays a role, sure. But how a student is treated once they're there? That's what counts more.

Let's be honest. For years, schools have leaned heavily on placement as the primary measure of inclusion. Still, what do we actually learn from that number? Does it tell us anything about how the student feels, or if they're even learning? If a student with a disability is in a general education classroom for 80% of the day, we check the box and move on. The box doesn't ask if they belong. It doesn't ask if they've made a friend or if they're part of the class conversation. It certainly doesn't ask if they're learning anything that is actually important to them.

This is often where we stop short. Placement is seen as the goal, not the beginning.

A stopwatch cannot measure real inclusion. Time in the room only tells us who was present, not what they experienced. What is worth the time is what happens while they're there. That means being known by your teacher, being missed when you're absent, and being part of something that feels real.

When teams sit down to discuss LRE at IEP meetings, the conversation usually starts and ends with placement options on a continuum. The list is familiar: general education, push-in, pull-out, special day class, maybe even a separate school. Sure, they're locations. But they tell us little about what the day actually feels like for the student inside. So what are we really asking when we talk about inclusion? Is it about being in the room, or being part of what's happening in it?

Sometimes a student is in the general education classroom, gets invited to join a group, and still ends up on the outside. The support is there, but it misses the mark. It doesn't match what that student needs in that moment. Inclusion rarely follows an either/or path. It emerges through small choices and patterns that create connection or reinforce separation.

We have to be careful not to confuse sameness with equity. The LRE isn't a universal destination. That decision is always personal. What feels inclusive for one student might feel overwhelming or isolating for another. That's why LRE has to be more than a number on a form. It has to reflect who the student is, what supports are in place, and where they're most likely to learn, connect, and grow.

That's the heart of the issue. Inclusion depends on how we teach, how we build relationships, and how we respond to student needs. It is not a passive process.

It doesn't start with big gestures. It starts with the way the classroom is structured. Things like how groups are formed, how support is shared, and how students are invited to contribute.

When that happens, students like Destiny start to take part in new ways. They ask questions, take the lead in small groups, and stop waiting for adults to speak on their behalf. They stop waiting for direction and start showing what they can do.

The benefits don't stop with her. The whole class gains something. Students learn that collaboration isn't about finding the fastest thinker. It's about listening, adapting, and creating ideas together. They learn that participation looks different for different people. They start to believe that everyone has something to offer, including themselves.

For teachers, it can feel overwhelming at first, because let's be real, it is. The long-term payoff is enormous. You start to see your students more clearly. You establish relationships that actually stick. Your classroom becomes a place where more kids feel safe, which means more kids are ready to learn.

None of this happens by accident.

So how do we move past inclusion that only looks good on paper?

It means paying attention to different things. Less about placement, more about experience. Rather than asking where a student is placed, we have to look at what their day actually feels like. Are they engaged? Are they learning? Do they feel like they belong?

Beyond Placement: What Progress Really Means

These questions are important, not just philosophically, but legally. In *Endrew F. v. Douglas County School District* (2017), the Supreme Court clarified that the goal of special education is more than minimal progress. IEPs must be "reasonably calculated to enable a child to make progress appropriate in light of the child's circumstances." That standard asks us to do better than the status quo. It pushes us to move beyond token presence in general education and instead focus on meaningful participation and growth.

And that doesn't happen through placement alone. It happens through practice.

In classrooms where inclusion works, support is a shared responsibility. The general education teacher isn't only aware of the IEP but actively involved in making it happen. They know the accommodations. They help design the modifications. As important, they value the student as a full member of the class.

One school I worked with had a standing weekly check-in between general and special education teachers. Fifteen minutes. That was it. They'd talk through how things went with shared students, swap ideas, and plan small changes. It wasn't formal. It wasn't extra paperwork. It was consistent. That small habit of checking in changed everything.

Another middle school teacher I know restructured group work by assigning rotating roles such as timekeeper, note-taker, speaker, and facilitator. Roles were assigned regardless of ability.

Everyone got a turn. That one shift led to more balanced participation, and over time, students who had previously hung back started stepping forward.

Even daily routines can change the atmosphere. One teacher started every day with a short community circle. A few minutes, one prompt, and a chance for each student to share. No pressure. No big production. Simply a habit of listening and being listened to. Students who used to feel invisible found their voice in those few minutes a day. What might change if we gave students a predictable moment to be heard, even for just five minutes a day?

Inclusion that works doesn't come from grand gestures. It grows through steady routines. Ones planned ahead, part of daily lessons, and consistent even on a chaotic day.

It might look as shown in Table 4.2.

These strategies are not about lowering expectations. They're about giving students the access and support they need to meet them.

That's what *Endrew F.* reminds us: progress isn't a bonus, it's the standard. Inclusion only works when students are engaged in learning, not simply occupying the same setting.

TABLE 4.2 Examples of Meaningful Participation

Scenario	*What It Looks Like*
Active Participation in Labs	A student with a reading goal works on a simplified version of a science lab, but still handles the materials, records observations, and shares findings with a peer. They're not simply sitting in. They're doing the lab, too.
Flexible Math Tasks	A teacher prepares two task versions for a math problem set. One uses manipulatives and real-world scenarios; the other involves open-ended challenge questions. All students work on the same concept, only with tools that match where they are.
Embedded IEP Goals	Instead of saving IEP goals for a pull-out session, a teacher targets them during regular instruction. If a student needs to practice writing complete sentences, that support is embedded in the writing block, not tacked on later.
Universal Supports	Supports like sentence frames, graphic organizers, and partner talk are used for everyone. They're not labeled or tracked. This normalizes support and reduces stigma.

Invisible No More

Here's a piece we don't talk about enough: the difference between being included and feeling like you belong.

Inclusion typically focuses on access. Things like who is physically in the room, on time spent in general education, on compliance with the IEP. But belonging is something else entirely. It's emotional and relational. It's the feeling that you are not only welcome but wanted. That you have a place, just as you are.

Students with disabilities have been saying it for years: inclusion is about relationships. It's about having friends, feeling like you're part of something, and not standing off to the side. When asked what makes them feel like they belong, students consistently point to connection. They don't mean merely being in the room. They mean being seen, being wanted, being with. In one study, students said they felt most included when they were treated like equals by peers, had real opportunities for friendship, and knew their presence made a difference (Arney & Rozek, 2024). That same message echoed across three countries in research by Little et al. (2022), where students with disabilities described friendship and acceptance as the heart of what it meant to feel included. The message was clear: without connection, inclusion feels hollow.

Unfortunately, for a lot of students, those relationships are still out of reach. They share a schedule, not a community. Carter and Hughes (2005) found that high schoolers with significant disabilities had far fewer chances to spend time with classmates. Most of their social interaction happened with adults or support staff, not other students. That's not belonging. That's solely being nearby. The TIES Center reports that even in classrooms labeled inclusive, students with significant disabilities can still be on the outside socially. Present, but not invited in. Carter and Biggs (2021) argue that building true communities of belonging for these students means rethinking not only instruction, but relationships. That's a staggering gap in belonging, especially in schools that claim to be inclusive.

This is more than a social issue. Belonging matters for learning and for a student's emotional well-being. Disconnection shows up in small ways: students pull back, stop trying, or lose interest altogether. In contrast, feeling valued, knowing you belong, makes it more likely a student will stay engaged and believe in their ability to succeed. Goodenow (1993) found that students who felt a stronger sense of belonging put more effort into school and were more focused. That still holds true. Belonging is the starting point. We cannot treat it as an add-on.

This brings us back to *Endrew F*. The Supreme Court's 2017 ruling established that students are entitled to an education that allows for "progress appropriate in light of the child's circumstances." That includes more than purely grades or test scores. If a student is eating alone every day, participating only with adult help, and never forming peer relationships, can we honestly say they are making meaningful progress? Are we meeting the spirit of the law, or just the letter?

In many cases, the barrier is not the student's disability but the environment around them. When students with disabilities are asked why they struggle socially, they often don't point to personal traits. They talk about classroom structure, lack of opportunities to engage, or simply not being invited to participate. These are factors we can change.

Inclusion or exclusion often shows up most clearly during lunch and recess. They're also some of the hardest times to structure well. While classrooms often follow a plan, unstructured time rarely does. For students with disabilities, that's when the social gaps can widen fast.

In many schools, students with disabilities are still eating alone or sitting only with their aides. Carter and Hughes (2005) observed that without intentional supports, students with severe disabilities often lacked opportunities to engage with their peers. But when teachers set up structured social groups, even something as simple as a weekly "Lunch Bunch," things shifted. Isolated students started making connections. Peers joined in eagerly. These weren't forced interactions. They were natural relationships sparked by a little structure and a little care.

Recess, too, can be rethought. Brock and colleagues have documented how students with disabilities, particularly those with social communication challenges, often linger at the edges of the playground. When schools introduced peer buddies or inclusion aides to help guide interactions, these same students became more engaged in play and conversation. They stopped hovering and started participating (Brock et al., 2020).

What this tells us is that belonging rarely happens on its own. It needs to be designed into the culture of the school.

That starts with educators. Teachers shape classroom norms. They decide who is called on, how groups are formed, and what kind of behavior is modeled and celebrated. Rubie-Davies (2010) found that students reported stronger self-belief and engagement when their teachers held high expectations for all learners and created a classroom climate that supported meaningful participation. In contrast, when students were routinely pulled out or supported by aides without being truly included, they often felt peripheral. Not because of the services themselves, but because of how those services were delivered.

Support staff also play a role. Paraeducators often walk a tightrope between helping a student and unintentionally separating them from their peers. Without clear guidance, it's easy to fall into patterns where the student is supported, but also isolated. Support doesn't need to be removed; it needs to be redesigned. Paraeducators need tools and coaching to know when to step forward and when to fade back. Especially during group work or social times, their presence should be a bridge to peer interaction, not a substitute for it.

The key idea is this: real inclusion isn't just about access. It's about connection. Belonging doesn't come from being in the room. It comes from being known, needed, and invited.

A Culture of Connection

Creating a culture of belonging can't fall on one teacher alone. While classroom practices have a place, the structure and climate of the entire school set the tone. When belonging is prioritized at a schoolwide level through peer supports, inclusive clubs, intentional planning around lunch and recess, and visible leadership from administrators, students notice. So do their families. What would it look like if every part of the school, from lunch to leadership, was designed for connection?

Some schools have adopted simple but powerful peer support systems. These can take many forms, from peer buddies to structured lunch groups to classwide cooperative learning roles. Programs like "Lunch Bunch" or "Circle of Friends" intentionally bring students together during less structured times of day. In a large randomized study, Carter et al. (2016) found that when students with significant disabilities were paired with trained peer partners during everyday routines, they experienced more social interaction, greater engagement, and real friendship gains. Students who had once eaten alone were suddenly part of something. And their peers? They showed up. That small act of invitation made a noticeable difference. Within weeks, those same students were chatting, laughing, and looking forward to lunchtime. What changed wasn't the students themselves. It was the environment.

Real belonging takes more than placing students in a room together. Long and Guo (2023) argue that while inclusion is a necessary step, it doesn't guarantee participation or emotional connection. Belonging requires something more. It means creating frameworks where students feel accepted, seen, and able to contribute in ways that are impactful to them. It's about feeling connected. Feeling part of something that feels real.

Extracurricular activities are another key area. Too often, students with disabilities are left out of clubs, sports, and other after-school opportunities. When schools create inclusive extracurriculars such as unified sports teams, inclusive theater groups, or buddy-led service clubs, those barriers start to fall away. The most effective programs are ones where students with and without disabilities participate side by side, with meaningful roles for everyone. These shared experiences build friendships and challenge assumptions.

Some schools also set aside dedicated student connection time during the week, often referred to as "advisory" or "morning meeting." These are short, nonacademic blocks led by a consistent adult, where students gather in small groups to check in, create community, or talk through social and emotional topics.

They give students room to be seen and heard outside of regular instruction. When used well, these meetings can strengthen peer connections and help identify students who may feel isolated. They also offer an opportunity to teach empathy, celebrate differences, and design shared classroom norms.

Leadership plays a major role in all of this. When principals and school leaders name belonging as a priority, when they model inclusive language, address exclusionary practices, and celebrate community-building efforts, they set a tone that ripples through the school. Students see it. Teachers feel supported in making time for these efforts. Families recognize the culture.

Of course, schoolwide efforts only work when they are matched by inclusive practices in the classroom. General education teachers play a central role in making sure that belonging is not something that only happens at recess or in clubs. It has to happen during instruction, too.

One approach is using cooperative learning structures where each student has a clearly defined role. These roles rotate regularly and are not assigned based on ability. When students with disabilities are given meaningful responsibilities and teammates rely on their input, it creates a culture of mutual respect. Instead of sitting on the sidelines, they take on meaningful roles and share responsibility with their peers.

Another effective practice is using whole-class routines that invite universal participation. These can include short partner talks, writing responses on whiteboards, sharing ideas in a poll, or using sentence starters so that every student has a way to contribute. These structures change the conversation from focusing on the fastest hand-raiser to creating opportunities for everyone's voice.

Instruction can also include varied entry points. Instead of giving every student the exact same task, teachers can offer different prompts or supports for the same concept. This is often called parallel tasking. When done well, students with disabilities work on the same big idea as their peers, but in a way that meets them where they are. The class stays together in purpose, even if the tools or steps look different.

Finally, teachers shape belonging through the language they use. When educators say things like, "Everyone learns differently here," or, "We all have something to offer," they send a message that difference is not something to be fixed. It's part of the fabric of the classroom.

Redesigning Destiny's Day

Let's end where we began, with Destiny.

On paper, her placement met the legal requirements. She was in her LRE. She sat in the general education classroom for most of the day. She had access to the curriculum and an instructional assistant to help her. But we know now that this was only a surface-level view. She occupied the same setting but wasn't really part of the class. Her experience didn't reflect meaningful inclusion, and it certainly didn't reflect belonging.

Now imagine her day in a different kind of school.

At lunch, she's part of a rotating table group, organized weekly by her teacher, not as a reward or punishment, but as a way to establish peer connections over time. One student in each group has a "host" role: they make sure everyone's included in the conversation. That tiny shift turns lunch from isolation into routine community-building.

Her paraeducator doesn't stay by her side. The paraeducator checks in with a few students, including Destiny, and quietly coaches her to ask a classmate before turning to an adult. There's a plan in place: when Destiny raises her hand during independent work, the assistant waits five seconds before responding, giving classmates a chance to step in first. It's subtle. But it works.

In science, Destiny joins a small group with preassigned roles: data recorder, materials handler, and presenter. The roles rotate each week, regardless of ability. Today, she's the one writing on the chart paper and explaining their hypothesis to the class. Tomorrow, someone else will take the lead.

Her general and special education teachers meet weekly. It may be only for 15 minutes, but they meet to check in on how shared students are doing. It's not formal, it's not written up. It's something that is consistent. That routine keeps her supports aligned with the reality of the classroom, not only what's on paper.

Inclusion isn't declared. It's designed. But designing it takes more than one teacher's effort. Belonging doesn't grow in isolation. It takes leadership that protects planning time, schedules that allow collaboration, and a school culture that values relationships as much as results. Teachers can plant the seeds, but the soil has to be ready too. And it shows up in how her day is designed, not just where she sits.

In that school, Destiny is not just supported. She is known. Her name is used in classroom discussions. Her ideas are written on the board. Her classmates ask her to join their group. She is invited to a birthday party. She is missed when she's absent. She is part of the community of the class.

That is what it looks like to move from access to connection. That is what it means to be in a school where belonging is part of the foundation.

This vision is not theoretical. It is grounded in what research shows us about the experiences of students with disabilities across age groups and contexts. It is supported by what students have told us again and again when asked directly. They want to learn. They want to have friends. They want to feel like they belong. And they want to be seen as more than the services they receive.

It's also what the law expects, even if the language doesn't always say it outright. In *Endrew F.*, the court reminded us that IEPs must aim for progress that is meaningful. That includes progress toward academic goals, but it also includes participation, interaction, confidence, and engagement. We cannot view these as add-ons. They are part of what defines a successful educational experience. And they are deeply connected to the way a student sees themselves in the world.

When schools take steps to create environments where every student feels like they belong, something shifts. Classrooms become more relational. Peers become more empathetic. Teachers become more responsive. And the students who once hovered at the edge of the group start to take their place inside of it.

This work isn't easy. It requires intention and collaboration. It often requires slowing down and noticing things that are easy to overlook: who is eating alone, who hasn't spoken today, who gets called on and who doesn't, who gets chosen for leadership roles, and who is always in the audience. Once you start seeing it, you can't unsee it. And once you name it, you can start to change it.

Belonging grows in the small, daily choices that teachers, paraeducators, administrators, and even peers make. It grows when we think about lunch and recess as learning spaces. When we train support staff to be connectors instead of buffers. When we embed participation into every lesson instead of saving it for certain students. When we listen to students, especially those who have been on the margins, and believe them when they tell us what helps and what hurts.

The idea of the LRE was never meant to be shorthand for inclusion. It was meant to be a safeguard, a starting point, a reminder to ensure students with disabilities have the right to learn and grow alongside their peers. That promise only counts if we're willing to go deeper than placement.

We ask better questions. Instead of asking, "Is she in general ed?" ask, "Who does she sit with at lunch?" "Who's in her reading group?" "Who notices when she's out sick?" Those are the moments that help us stop talking about inclusion as a legal term and start building it into the life of the school.

Isn't that what school should be? A place where every student feels seen, known, and needed.

When we get that right, students like Destiny don't just show up for attendance. They show up as themselves, and the classroom is better because they're in it.

References

Arney, M., & Rozek, C. (2024). *Fostering school belonging for students in special education*. PRiME Center, St. Louis University. https://www.primecenter.org/education-reports-database/school-belonging

Brock, M. E., Carter, E. W., & Biggs, E. E. (2020). Supporting peer interactions, relationships, and belonging. In F. Brown, J. McDonnell, & M. E. Snell (Eds.), *Instruction of students with severe disabilities* (9th ed., pp. 384–417). Merrill.

Carter, E. W., Asmus, J., Moss, C. K., Biggs, E. E., Bolt, D. M., Born, T. L., Brock, M. E., Cattey, G. N., Chen, R., Cooney, M., Fesperman, E., Hochman, J. M., Huber, H. B., Lequia, J. L., Lyons, G., Moyseenko, K. A., Riesch, L. M., Shalev, R. A., Vincent, L. B., & Weir, K. (2016). Randomized evaluation of peer support arrangements to support the inclusion of high school students with severe disabilities. *Exceptional Children*, *82*(2), 209–233. https://doi.org/10.1177/0014402915598780

Carter, E. W., & Biggs, E. E. (2021). *Creating communities of belonging for students with significant cognitive disabilities (belonging series)*. University of Minnesota, TIES Center.

Carter, E. W., & Hughes, C. (2005). Increasing social interaction among adolescents with autism spectrum disorders in inclusive classrooms: Effective instructional strategies. *Research and Practice for Persons with Severe Disabilities*, *30*(4), 179–193. https://doi.org/10.2511/rpsd.30.4.179

Endrew F. v. Douglas County School District RE-1, 580 U.S. 137 (2017).

Goodenow, C. (1993). Classroom belonging among early adolescent students: Relationships to motivation and achievement. *The Journal of Early Adolescence*, *13*(1), 21–43. https://doi.org/10.1177/0272431693013001002

Little, C., de Leeuw, R. R., Andriana, E., Zanuttini, J., & Evans, D. (2022). Social inclusion through the eyes of the student: Perspectives from students with disabilities on friendship and acceptance. *International Journal of Disability, Development and Education*, *69*(6), 2074–2093. https://doi.org/10.1080/1034912X.2020.1837352

Long, T., & Guo, J. (2023). Moving beyond inclusion to belonging. *International Journal of Environmental Research and Public Health*, 20(6907). https://doi.org/10.3390/ijerph20206907

Rubie-Davies, C. M. (2010). Teacher expectations and perceptions of student attributes: Is there a relationship? *British Journal of Educational Psychology*, *80*(1), 121–135. https://doi.org/10.1348/000709909X466334

5

Justice for All

Culture, Identity, and the Inclusive Classroom

Education isn't neutral. It reflects the history, values, and power structures of the society that created it. Special education is no exception. It has never existed in a vacuum.

Walk into any classroom, you'll see it. Culture shows up in the language students use, how they connect, the stories they bring from home, and the values that shape their day. Too often, systems ignore these realities. We can't afford that anymore if we want schools to work for all kids.

For years, most conversations circled around on eligibility, services, and individual needs. Those concerns are real, but they miss what surrounds a student. Race, language, culture, and community influence how adults see them, which influences what support is offered, how concerns are interpreted, and whether strengths are recognized.

We already looked at how these patterns began in Chapter 1, but they haven't ended. Students do not experience special education equally. Those disparities aren't random. In the early days, students of color were left out or placed in programs labeled "educable mentally retarded." Those decisions rested on flawed assumptions and racially biased IQ tests. Court cases like *Larry P. v. Riles* (1986) and *Diana v. State Board of Education* (1970) pushed back, but the impact didn't disappear. The same biases that shaped discipline and treatment in general education showed up in labels and placements. That history still affects how students are seen today, especially where race, language, and disability overlap.

Those legacies show up now in subtle ways. In referrals, in whose behavior is tolerated, in how compliance is valued over curiosity. Teachers and administrators may not mean to exclude, but without a critical lens, the system replicates itself.

Students of color, particularly Black, Latino, and Indigenous students, along with multilingual learners, are identified more often in certain disability categories. They are also placed in more restrictive settings and disciplined at higher rates. This isn't only about numbers. Still, the numbers tell the story. About 15% of all students get special education services, but the rate is higher for Black students (17%) and Native American students (19%) (Barrio & Allen, 2024; U.S. Department of Education, 2023).

They also miss out on enrichment, leadership opportunities, advanced coursework. Black students make up 15% of school-aged youth but only 9% of gifted enrollment. In communities with higher anti-Black bias, they are less likely to be placed in gifted programs even when achievement looks the same (Pearman & McGee, 2022). These patterns don't happen by chance. They reflect how systems respond to assumptions about who a student is and what they might become.

Ignoring these patterns only reinforces them.

Culture matters. It has always been part of special education, whether we named it or not. It needs to show up in how we see students, how we make decisions, and how we build support. That includes the assumptions we have, the stories we believe, and the patterns we've stopped noticing. That's the work: challenging what we call normal and seeing students more fully.

Seeing with New Eyes

Disability isn't seen the same way in every community. For some families, it is a medical issue. For others, a spiritual matter or a social burden. That caution comes from experience. Families remember how their kids have been treated in school, in healthcare, in every system. What might look like hesitation to an educator could be a parent protecting their child from more harm.

Misidentification doesn't always come from malice. Often, it is about tools never planned for the students using them. Mohamed (2023) found, in a study of immigrant families, that culturally and linguistically diverse students were flagged for special education after struggling with English, not learning itself. Families described evaluations they couldn't understand, meetings they couldn't participate in, services never explained in their language. One mother didn't even know her daughter had been receiving special education until months later.

The study named three themes: inaccurate screenings, grade retention, lack of parent awareness. That pattern isn't a simple testing error. It is a systems issue, happening most to students whose families are least prepared, or least invited, to push back.

When a parent questions a referral, it doesn't mean they oppose support. It might mean they don't trust what's on offer.

Immigrant families often arrive with different beliefs about what schools can or should provide. In some countries, students with disabilities are excluded from public education. In others, there is little formal support. They bring their own sense of what a label means, what services exist, and what it might cost socially or emotionally to accept them.

Language differences add more layers. A student still learning English may struggle in class. Is it a language gap? A teaching mismatch? Or something else? We ask whether challenges come from limited English proficiency, which is important. But if instruction hasn't been adapted to support language development, it can look like disability when what the student really needs is better access. For families new to the system, or handling it in a second language, it is hard to know what to ask or how to advocate.

Black communities hold reasons to be cautious too. Disproportionate placement, harsher discipline, and restrictive settings are not new. They are patterns. Families who have seen that up close aren't showing mistrust. They are showing a learned response.

All of this sits in a deep history of harm and survival. When educators overlook that context, even good intentions can do damage. That's why culturally responsive practice is more than helpful. It is protective.

Seeing the Student, Not Just the Behavior

These disparities don't only show up in spreadsheets. They surface in small moments. Referrals, evaluations, the supports students receive or don't. A teacher might flag a student because something feels "off," when the problem is a mismatch between the student's learning and the classroom's structure. When we fail to see that, we read difference as a problem.

For Black and Latino boys, especially, frustration or boredom can get read as disrespect or emotional disturbance. Instead of asking what sits underneath, we respond with discipline or a new label. That can mean a more restrictive placement, a pattern that sticks,

Students from historically marginalized communities are often left out of gifted programs. It isn't about ability. Their strengths may show up in ways schools don't expect. A student who pushes beyond the lesson, who connects ideas or spots problems no one named yet, might never get identified as gifted if those skills don't match tests or classroom norms.

What some adults see as defiance can actually be boredom. A student who seems tuned out might not be trying to cause problems. They might need more challenge. When we slow down and ask different questions, ones centered on possibility, the story changes.

I once worked with a gifted education teacher who saw a troubling pattern. Black kindergarten boys were written up repeatedly for refusing directions or "talking back" during lessons. Instead of filing behavior referrals, she started screening them for gifted programs. Nearly all qualified. What some described as defiance was really a mismatch between classroom demands and student needs. If no one had looked closer, those students might have been given a label that followed them for years.

Multilingual learners face similar risks. A student still learning English might be skipped over for enrichment because their strengths aren't visible in familiar ways. They could be making connections, solving problems, and staying engaged, only not in English yet. If assessments and conversations focus on one language, those skills slip under the radar. What is part of language acquisition can look like a learning delay. That's how a student ends up in a special education program that doesn't match their needs.

These decisions have long-term consequences. The moment a student is labeled, it can change how teachers interact with them, what opportunities they are offered, and how peers see them. None of this depends on ability. It depends on how we define success, how we respond to difference, and whether we are willing to examine the systems that influence those choices.

Resilience Shouldn't Be the Requirement

Educators have started to rethink how they talk about resilience, especially when a student overcomes long odds to succeed. These stories remind us of what young people can achieve, but also of what they were pushed to endure just to be recognized. Before we celebrate resilience, we have to ask why it was needed in the first place. When we ignore the conditions that made survival necessary, we end up praising students for enduring a system that should have served them better.

I truly don't believe there's any such thing as a self-made success story. Every person has a history. Sometimes support was offered. Other times, opportunities were missed, or systems fell short. Resilience does not appear out of nowhere. It often grows in response to conditions that should never have existed. When those conditions are structural, toughness should not be the lesson we celebrate.

I have seen far too many stories, especially about adults, framed around toughness and perseverance. What they really needed was someone who noticed what they were going through. Celebrating these stories without asking about the cost sends the message that survival is the goal and toughness is what we value most. It suggests that if you didn't make it, you simply weren't strong enough.

Strength-based work should help us question what created the struggle. Naming students' assets should also push us to ask what created the struggle in the first place. If we move beyond admiring how students cope and ask why they had to, we get closer to changing the conditions that demanded resilience.

Culturally responsive practice helps us rethink how we see students and create spaces where school feels welcoming, not something to survive.

What Makes Learning Stick

Bias and inequity show up in how students get identified. That's only the starting point. From there, it comes down to how we teach, how we connect, and how we design classrooms that honor who students are. Culturally responsive practice begins with trust. Without it, there is no real learning.

What do students really need to engage, not merely comply, but truly show up as learners? Zaretta Hammond talks about learning as both cultural and neurological (Hammond, 2015). For students to fully take part, they need to feel safe, connected, and challenged in ways that make sense to them. When that doesn't happen, especially for kids who already sense school was never set up with them in mind, their brains do what they're supposed to do. Their brains protect them by holding back and shutting down. It is no surprise that students stop participating.

Special education adds another layer. Labels shape how others see a student, what they expect, and what they plan for. If instruction ignores a student's culture or skips over their experiences, the chance to establish a real learning partnership gets lost.

This Isn't New Work

The need for this kind of instruction isn't new. Back in 1994, Gloria Ladson-Billings laid out one of the clearest pictures of what culturally relevant teaching can actually look like in *The Dreamkeepers* (Ladson-Billings, 1994/2022). In the 2022 edition, she revisits that work and reminds us that the core ideas still hold up, maybe even more now than before. She followed teachers who were doing it well. Teachers who knew how to connect with Black students without lowering the bar. What she found came down to three things: academic success, cultural competence, and critical consciousness. These teachers saw their students for who they were and expected them to think critically, not only about the content, but about the world around them. They pushed students to grow, but never at the expense of where they came from or what they were experiencing. That balance between affirmation and accountability is still one of the clearest paths toward equity we have.

Hammond (2015) describes culturally responsive teaching as the process of helping students become independent learners by building their capacity to process and retain information. That starts with trust, but not the vague kind. She outlines a set of "trust generators." These are small, intentional actions that signal respect and care. These include things like showing selective vulnerability, using personal talk to connect, and being warm demanders who combine high expectations with strong relationships. In other words, students need to know they're safe before they can stretch. They also need to know that the adults around them believe they can grow.

It's Going to Be Uncomfortable

Of course, that kind of trust goes both ways. For educators, leaning into culturally responsive practice can feel risky, especially when you worry about getting it wrong. Most of us were never trained to talk about culture, much less teach through it. Mistakes happen. You might misread a moment or say something that lands differently than you meant, or have a student repeat your words in a way that stirs up confusion or tension at home. That fear is real. For many teachers, it can be enough to pull away from these conversations altogether.

Culturally responsive instruction asks us to stay with it anyway. It means asking deeper questions about your students, their families, and even yourself. That kind of openness doesn't come from a script or a checklist. It grows from community, from a genuine sense of curiosity and care. What creates trust is being willing to learn out loud, to model that same vulnerability in your classroom, and to keep trying even when you get it wrong.

More Than Just Feeling Seen

From there, instruction has to do more than reflect culture. It has to activate it. That means intentionally linking new content to students' background knowledge and experiences. Hammond (2015) calls this creating the "schema." Specifically, this is helping students connect what they're learning to what they already know. That might mean choosing examples that speak to how students actually experience the world. This is not simply swapping in different names or holidays, but building from the realities they bring with them into the room. It could sound like using language that feels familiar or explaining something in a way that mirrors how ideas are talked about at home. Content should include students in ways that actually make sense to them. Yes, representation is important. Even more important is whether students feel like they're part of the learning, not watching it happen around them. Culture helps students make meaning. It gives them something solid to lean on when they're learning something new.

Hammond (2015) also talks about the power of scaffolded routines, which offer regular, structured chances for students to process what they're learning, think it through, and practice skills like comparing, categorizing, or summarizing. For students in special education, that steady kind of mental rehearsal can be huge. It helps foster independence without watering down the work. It also helps students see themselves as thinkers, not just as kids who need support.

In real classrooms, this kind of cultural grounding can take a lot of different forms. It might sound like a call-and-response moment integrated into a lesson, especially if that kind of interaction already feels natural to students. It might show up in sentence frames that reflect how students talk with each other outside of school, or in stories that connect with how they make sense of things in their own lives. A math problem might connect to a family business, a local event, or something students already interact with in their everyday lives. None of this has to be complicated. It mostly has to start with what's real and familiar. These shifts don't require a brand-new curriculum. They begin with listening and learning how your students move through the world.

For educators who don't share their students' cultural background, this work can feel uncomfortable at first. It should. There's a difference between honoring culture and performing it. The goal is not to imitate students' lives, but to build bridges between those lives and the content being taught. That starts with humility. It means asking more questions than giving answers, staying open to feedback, and being willing to get it wrong and try again.

Culturally responsive teaching isn't about performance. It's about relationship, relevance, and rebuilding trust in a system that hasn't always earned it.

When I look back on my time as a student, I can name quite a few teachers I felt connected to. Some of them didn't look like me, and they didn't sound like me either, but I still felt as though they noticed me. What made the difference wasn't some perfectly planned strategy. It was their willingness to take a real interest in the things that mattered to me.

There's one moment I still remember from early in high school. My English teacher had designated time for free reading, and we could pick whatever we wanted. I was reading Langston Hughes, and one day she asked me what I knew about the Harlem Renaissance. I didn't know much at the time. But her question got me thinking. I started asking more questions, digging a little deeper. Eventually, that became one of my favorite time periods in history. I doubt she saw it as culturally responsive teaching, but it felt like she was trying to connect with me over something I actually cared about. That made me care more, about the book, the class, and my own voice as a reader.

Ladson-Billings (2022) and Hammond (2015) are working from somewhat different angles, but the message could not be more aligned. It's more than helping students feel seen. It's about creating classrooms where they think critically, grow academically, and stay connected to who they are.

Culturally responsive teaching doesn't replace Individualized Education Program (IEP) goals or instructional accommodations. What it can do is strengthen them. It creates a context in which learning can actually take root. One where the student feels seen and supported, and where their id entity is a source of strength rather than a barrier to overcome.

This also applies to how we evaluate students. Standardized tests can give us some information, but they were never designed to see everything a student can do. Most of those tests use big national samples for comparison, which is fine for some purposes, yet they often miss the cultural or language factors that affect how kids show what they know. When we read scores without considering those differences, we can end up misunderstanding a student's needs or missing their strengths. A culturally responsive approach doesn't toss out standardized data, but puts it alongside other ways of knowing. That includes classroom performance, student and family input, and an understanding of how cultural background might shape how a student shows what they know.

Too often, cultural responsiveness is treated like a to-do list item in a larger process. Yet this work asks more of us. It calls for a reevaluate of how we think about teaching, learning, and support, seeing them not as separate efforts but as part of one system where culture isn't an add-on; it's at the center. When classrooms reflect who students are and respond to what they bring with them, inclusion stops being a checklist and starts becoming real.

This Is Their Story Too

When we talk about equity in special education, we often focus on school-based solutions. Things like instructional strategies, assessments, placements. But real change doesn't happen in isolation. It happens when the people most impacted by these decisions are included in shaping them.

Parents bring a kind of knowledge that can't be pulled from school records or progress reports. They see patterns, notice things others might miss, and often know what their child needs before anyone else does. That insight often gets overlooked, especially when there are cultural or communication differences. It's on us to make sure families know their input is equally important, not only during the meeting, but throughout the whole process. That starts with listening and being open to the possibility that parents might understand something we haven't figured out yet.

In a qualitative study (Goodwin et al., 2024), parents were asked what culturally responsive practices actually looked and felt like in their children's schools. The responses were more revealing than the questions. Families noticed when culture was treated like an afterthought. They noticed when schools failed to ask the right questions, or worse, asked but didn't really listen. One parent described it this way: "They are aware; they choose to ignore it."

That line captures something educators don't always want to admit, and that is that awareness is not the problem. The disconnect comes later, when good intentions don't translate into action, when culture is acknowledged in theory but not reflected in instruction, or partnerships, or policy. What parents described wasn't a lack of information. It was a lack of follow-through.

Establishing trust starts with listening. This is easier than it sounds. Many of us think we are listening, but really we are listening to respond or to persuade, not necessarily listening to understand. When we skip that step, we miss what families are actually trying to tell us. Real listening means setting aside our own agenda for a moment and being willing to hear something that might challenge what we thought we knew. It means asking follow-up questions, checking our assumptions, and paying attention to what's not being said, too.

Creating space for families starts with intention. Communication should happen in the languages families speak, as this is a requirement. Meetings should be accessible, both in format and timing. Connection shouldn't be limited to a once-a-year IEP meeting. To develop a genuine partnership, schools have to take the lead in creating trust. That includes acknowledging historical harm, offering multiple ways for families to engage, and designing processes that invite, not pressure, collaboration.

The goal is to design something better together, not simply respond to where families happen to be in the moment. It means moving forward with them.

Family engagement goes beyond only showing up for scheduled meetings. It grows out of relationships sustained over time, grounded in trust and shared purpose. That kind of connection makes it easier to ask hard questions, raise concerns, and work through disagreement. It also means we have to be honest about the power dynamics in the room. Do families feel like equal partners in the process? Is that something we talk about openly as a team? Also, how are we creating opportunities for their voices to influence decisions, not just echo them?

Schools can take steps to change that dynamic in real ways. Inviting families to help set the agenda for meetings, using clear and accessible language in all communication, and checking in outside of formal processes can all create more balanced and respectful partnerships. Creating outlets for families to speak first, reflect on their hopes and concerns, or even lead parts of the discussion sends a clear message: their voice is not only welcome, it is necessary.

Students should have a say in the decisions that affect their learning. In special education, they're often left out. Plans get written, meetings happen, and the student isn't even in the room, or if they are, no one's really asking for their input. Even small adjustments in how we include students can open the door to something better. Asking a student what helps them focus, what gets in their way, or what kind of support actually works for them can change the whole conversation. It helps them feel like part of the process, not simply someone being talked about.

This kind of engagement is often assumed to be appropriate only for older students, but elementary students are as capable of contributing. Their input might come in the form of drawings, short interviews, or conversations with a trusted adult. They might not yet have the vocabulary to name every need, but they can still tell us how they feel about school, what feels hard, and what makes them feel successful. When we place those check-ins into the process, it does more than amplify student voice.

It reduces the amount of resilience we expect kids to possess simply to be okay in school.

Developing student voice takes time. A kindergartener might choose between two learning activities or explain what helps them concentrate, while a high schooler might take an active role in an IEP meeting or advocate for a specific support. These kinds of skills don't only show up. They grow when students get chances to practice, reflect, and talk with adults who take them seriously.

One way educators can support this is by checking in with students regularly, teaching simple ways to name what they need, and modeling how to talk about challenges without judgment. It's in those small moments that students start to see their perspective as something that actually is important.

Supporting student voice means helping them find the language and confidence to talk about their learning. It also means creating environments where those conversations are welcomed. When students speak, adults need to listen, not only out of courtesy, but because what they say should influence how we respond.

Families, communities, and students bring knowledge that schools cannot manufacture. When that knowledge is ignored, we miss out on some of the most valuable insights we could have. And when it's invited in, we move one step closer to an education system that sees all students clearly, not as problems to be fixed but as people with stories that deserve to be heard.

Guardians of the Beginning

Equity in special education isn't a destination. It's a constant recalibration of how we see students, how we build relationships, and how we respond to difference with care instead of control. It starts with real questions. The kind we actually ask ourselves in those moments. What's this student trying to tell me? Am I missing something? Is there anything I haven't asked yet? It means slowing down and really listening, especially when the voices we need to hear aren't always the loudest ones in the room.

When we take the opportunity for students and families to share what they know, and we treat that input like it is important, it changes the narrative. It changes how school feels. We move away from systems established on compliance and toward spaces rooted in trust. That kind of change doesn't happen in a single meeting or moment. It happens through everyday choices. Who we invite into the conversation. What we choose to question. What we're willing to change.

Of course, none of this work happens alone. Collaboration is part of the fabric of inclusive education, and we'll be returning to it in more detail in later chapters. Because doing this well doesn't only take good intentions. It also takes a resilient team.

First, we need to talk about timing. Many of the biggest missed opportunities for equity happen well before a student is ever referred. The strongest interventions aren't reactive. They're thoughtful, proactive, and part of the classroom from the start.

So that's where we're headed next: how we support students before they get overlooked. How we recognize strengths before they get mislabeled as struggles. How early guardianship becomes one of the most powerful tools we have to revise the story before it's written for them.

References

Barrio, B. L., & Allen, C. D. (2024). Addressing disproportionality and racial inequities in special education through policy change. *Theory Into Practice*, *63*(4), 377–389. https://doi.org/10.1080/00405841.2024.2355819

Diana v. State Board of Education, No. C-70 37 RFP (N.D. Cal. 1970).

Goodwin, A. K. B., Long, A. C. J., Vasquez, J., Allouche, S. F., & Boatner, K. (2024). "They are aware; They choose to ignore it": The state of culturally responsive school practices through the Lens of parents. *School Psychology*. Advance online publication. https://doi.org/10.1037/spq0000641

Hammond, Z. (2015). *Culturally responsive teaching and the brain: Promoting authentic engagement and rigor among culturally and linguistically diverse students*. Corwin.

Ladson-Billings, G. (2022). *The dreamkeepers: Successful teachers of African American children* (2nd ed.). Jossey-Bass. (Original work published 1994)

Larry P. v. Riles, 793 F.2d 969 (9th Cir. 1986).

Mohamed, A. A. (2023). *Dis-labeling the ables: The overrepresentation of culturally and linguistically diverse students receiving special education services. Journal of Underrepresented and Minority Progress, 7*(1), 112–125. https://doi.org/10.32674/jump.v7i1.5010

Pearman, F. A. I. I., & McGee, E. O. (2022). Anti-blackness and racial disproportionality in gifted education. *Exceptional Children, 88*(4), 359–380. https://doi.org/10.1177/00144029211073523

U.S. Department of Education, Office of Special Education and Rehabilitative Services. (2023). *45th Annual Report to Congress on the Implementation of the Individuals with Disabilities Education Act*, 2023. https://sites.ed.gov/idea/files/45th-arc-for-idea.pdf

6

The Power of Early Guardianship

Proactive Support for Future Heroes

I imagine there's a moment in nearly every educator's career when they realize they could've done more if they had noticed what was happening a little sooner. A student starts falling behind. Not because they're unmotivated or incapable, but because the support they needed didn't show up in time. By the time someone acts, the gap has grown wide enough to be named: a diagnosis, a placement, a referral. Once it has a name, it's easy to forget how different it could have been.

Early intervention gets talked about a lot, but not always in the right way. We tend to treat it like a program or a checklist, mostly for preschoolers or kindergarteners who are already showing big, obvious signs of struggle. Early isn't just about age; it's about timing. It means noticing "before it gets harder." Before confidence erodes. Before school becomes a place a student wants to escape. Before adults decide, the only option left is a label.

So what does "harder" actually look like?

Take Mateo, for example. In first grade, he was the kid who always had to go to the bathroom during writing time. Every single day, right when it was time to pick up a pencil, he'd raise his hand. Sometimes he'd pretend to sharpen his pencil three or

TABLE 6.1 Two Paths for Supporting Mateo

Scenario	Description
Scenario 1: The Moment Passes	No one notices the pattern. Mateo gets a little more frustrated each day. His writing folder starts coming home empty. He's marked as "off task" on the report card. By second grade, writing time is a full-on battle. He tells the teacher it's boring. He tells his mom it hurts his hand. He starts acting out just enough to get sent to the hallway, which, frankly, feels better than failing. Eventually, someone raises the idea of ADHD. Maybe a referral for occupational therapy. Then maybe a 504 plan. A whole lot of labels get tossed around. Meanwhile, Mateo's confidence keeps dwindling.
Scenario 2: Someone Notices	A reading specialist stops by during an observation and notices something the teacher hadn't. Mateo isn't seen as only squirmy. He doesn't know how to hold a pencil properly. Writing isn't something that is simply frustrating; it's physically uncomfortable. No one had asked, so no one had known. A few weeks of occupational therapy support, paired with some basic fine motor practice during morning stations, makes a huge difference. But the part that brings the biggest smile to the teacher isn't the improved writing. It's that Mateo stays in the room during writing time. He even asks to share his story with the class.

four times in a row. The teacher, kind and patient, assumed he was simply wiggly. Maybe even a little avoidant.

Here's how that moment can unfold in two very different ways (Table 6.1).

Two paths for the same student, in the same classroom, with the same teacher. One outcome came from waiting. The other came from noticing before things got harder.

This is what we mean by early. Early means paying attention to when support is needed, not how old a student is. A choice to respond before a student starts to internalize struggle as failure. Before we start talking about what's "wrong." Early guardianship doesn't require a referral, a meeting, or a plan. It starts with noticing and asking different questions.

This isn't about holding off until things fall apart or a diagnosis arrives. We're building habits and systems that make early support possible, without needing hindsight to guide us. That means noticing patterns before they become problems, responding before confidence wears down, and rethinking what kind of help students need and when they need it.

You won't find any big dramatic rescues here. Most of the work happens behind the scenes, but it doesn't happen in isolation. These kinds of supports are often the result of shared planning, real-time conversations, and a school culture where teachers feel safe enough to ask questions, try something new, and figure things out together. A teacher who tapes simple checklists to a student's desk so they don't have to keep asking what to do next. A school that designs small group instruction into their schedule for everyone, not only the kids who are behind. A counselor who turns an old storage closet into a sensory-friendly retreat that students can visit without a pass or a story.

We'll get into Multi-Tiered System of Supports (MTSS). Not because it's trendy or required, but because when it's done well, it creates a structure for this kind of early support to happen regularly and without stigma. The point isn't to memorize tiers. The point is to respond before a student's need becomes a reason to remove them.

By the time a student is referred to special education, the story is already complicated. And not all of it has been supportive. If we really want to reduce over-identification, if we really want fewer students internalizing the message that they are the problem, then we have to stop confusing eligibility with need. Not every struggle needs a label, but every student needs to be seen.

That's what early guardianship is. It's noticing the small stuff. It's choosing to act early, even when it would be easier to wait and see. It's believing that a student's path doesn't need to be shaped by failure before it can be shaped by support.

Noticing Before It Becomes a Struggle

Early intervention is often treated like a formal step in a process. Something that begins with paperwork, protocols, or a flagged score. The real beginning comes earlier. It starts when someone pays attention. When a teacher notices a pattern that doesn't quite line up with what's expected. Not to correct or punish, but simply to understand what's happening.

Sometimes that pattern is academic: a student who avoids rhyming games or can't seem to hold onto letter sounds no matter how many times they're reviewed. Other times it's social: a child who hangs around the carpet of group time, never quite joining in. They might not join in, not due to lack of interest, but because the how isn't yet clear to them. Or it's behavioral: a student who always has something to say, who interrupts often, challenges directions, and seems to push back on nearly everything. Not because they're trying to be defiant, but because they process out loud and need space to feel heard.

None of these moments, in isolation, is enough to trigger a referral. And that's exactly why they're often overlooked. Struggles don't usually arrive all at once. They start gradually, piece by piece, until a fuller picture starts to take shape. By that point, the student may already believe they're the problem. We saw this with Mateo. What seemed like avoidance was actually discomfort. A pattern that first looked like restlessness turned out to be something else entirely. Once someone took the time to notice, everything began to change. That's the real power of early support. It meets students in that in-between space, before the struggle becomes a story they internalize. It helps them feel capable before they start to question whether they are. It says, "We see you," before they start to feel like no one notices them.

This doesn't always require a full-blown plan or a formal team. Sometimes it's a small shift in classroom routines that makes the biggest difference. One classroom strategy with a long track record of success is the Good Behavior Game (GBG). First developed in 1969, it's been studied for decades across grade levels and settings. Students are grouped into teams, and during instructional time, they earn points for meeting class expectations. When the team meets a set goal, they get a simple reward. This could be something like extra recess or a class privilege. It's easy to set up, doesn't require anything fancy, and can run in the background of regular instruction.

A recent study found that teachers using a strengths-focused version of the GBG not only saw increases in academic engagement but also reported significantly lower levels of stress at the end of the school day (Radley et al., 2024). That part is essential because strategies like this don't only help students thrive, they also help the adults breathe.

One piece that often gets lost in all the forms, timelines, and data meetings is this: kids know when they're struggling. They might not have the words for it, but they feel it. They see it in the way their classmates finish faster. In the way their name comes up during behavior talks. In the sigh a teacher doesn't mean to let out. They start to internalize the idea that something is off. If we don't intervene early with real support, not only redirection, that belief can stick harder than the skill deficit ever did.

This is why early intervention has to be strengths-based. It cannot focus only on what a student cannot do. That kind of framing becomes its own kind of barrier. A student who struggles with handwriting might be an incredible storyteller. Give them a speech-to-text app, and suddenly the story flows. A child who melts down during transitions might have a strong need for predictability. Add a visual schedule or a short preview of what's coming next, and the meltdowns start to fade. The need doesn't disappear, but it becomes manageable. It becomes something the student can navigate instead of something they're punished for.

We've seen this across all kinds of needs. Students with dyslexia often make significant gains with structured literacy approaches. But they also thrive when they're allowed to read about things that actually interest them, even if it's through audiobooks or graphic novels. Kids with processing disorders might need more time, not less challenge. Students with ADHD might do better when they're allowed to stand, move, create, and question. These strategies might not match traditional expectations, yet they support engagement all the same.

Support gets better when it's grounded in understanding, not urgency. It means creating the kind of support that helps students access learning, without sending the message that needing help is the same as falling behind. Too often, schools operate like a kitchen in the middle of a dinner rush. People start grabbing whatever's closest, tossing ingredients together, and hoping something edible ends up on the plate. There's no recipe, no prep time, and definitely no chance to step back and ask what we're trying to make.

When systems are planned instead of patched together, everyone understands their role, the tools they have, and what success is supposed to look like. There's time to learn, time to practice, and time to get better. That kind of structure doesn't only help students succeed. It shows adults what it looks like to work in a culture that values preparation, not only quick fixes. Because teachers aren't improvisers holding things together with tape. They're skilled professionals, and they deserve systems built with the same care we want them to give their students.

One of the most common misconceptions in education is that support has to come with a label. That a student has to be diagnosed before they can be helped. But that's backward, most of what works for students with identified needs also works for students who haven't been formally identified yet or who may never be. You don't need a diagnosis to benefit from clarity, connection, or kindness.

This doesn't mean throwing out structure or lowering expectations. Early intervention is actually about raising them, and giving students the tools they need to meet high standards. It's about creating momentum early so that success becomes the story they tell themselves instead of struggle. When we wait until students are already behind, already discouraged, already disconnected, we haven't intervened. We've simply reacted, and reaction is not the same as support.

When Support Becomes a System

There's only so much one teacher can do. Observation, creativity, and flexibility are essential, but they're not a replacement for schoolwide systems that make support consistent and accessible. The reality is that good instincts aren't always enough. Even the best teachers miss things when the load is too heavy or the structures around them aren't built to respond.

This is where schools often fall short. Not because they don't care, but because they haven't built a process for what happens next. A student shows signs of struggling, and everything depends on whether the right person notices, has time to act, and knows what to do. If no one steps in, the moment passes, the pattern grows, and what might have been manageable early on turns into something far more complex and difficult to address.

Early intervention works best when it's part of something bigger, something more than a collection of individual strategies. It depends on a shared approach to how schools respond to student needs. One that treats support as a regular part of school life rather than an exception. In these systems, students are seen early, helped early, and supported without stigma.

This doesn't require new programs or extra staff. It starts with consistency. A common language for how teachers flag concerns. A process for checking in on students who are showing early signs of struggle. A plan for what kind of help comes first, and how that support can be adapted if things don't improve. In places where this kind of system exists, you can feel the difference. Teachers don't feel like they're guessing. Students don't have to fail before they get help. And families are brought in early, not only when a referral is on the table. In those schools, support becomes something shared. Something schools do with students, not for them.

At one school, it started with a clipboard.

Each grade-level team kept one. Nothing fancy, it was simply a list of student names with a few columns to jot quick notes. Teachers used it during weekly planning to flag small things they noticed. Cameron is crying every morning before drop-off. Jaelynn is hiding her math work under her desk. Elijah hasn't turned in a writing assignment in two weeks, even though he's finishing everything else.

The point wasn't to diagnose, determine eligibility, or jump to solutions. It was a way to track what teachers were already noticing and see if anything started to add up.

On their own, those observations might not have led anywhere; however, pulled together, the pattern was easier to spot. If one teacher noticed a student shutting down during writing, and someone else had seen the same thing during science, that was worth noting. It didn't mean there was a problem; it meant the student was on their radar.

Cameron's anxiety started showing up in other classes too. The counselor stepped in early and started Check-In/Check-Out (CICO). These were brief daily check-ins with the same adult, which was enough consistency to keep him from having a difficult time before the first period. Jaelynn wasn't engaging in math at all, so her teacher started using dry erase response boards during warm-ups. Everyone held up their thinking at once, no pressure to speak out loud. She started participating again. When Elijah began missing writing assignments, the reading specialist noticed something: he could tell the story fine when he talked, but couldn't get it down on paper. They added voice dictation during writing blocks. That Monday he turned in three pieces of writing he hadn't been able to complete in weeks.

This wasn't a big, formal intervention plan, nor were these dramatic changes. They were the kind of small moments that happen when teachers are supported and systems are set up to catch what we often miss. That clipboard didn't solve everything, but it helped people pay attention to the right things at the right time. That was enough to change the trajectory for a few students who might have otherwise slipped through.

Laying the Groundwork for Systemic Support

When we talk about support, it's easy to picture a handful of teachers doing their best with limited time and a growing list of needs. That's the unfortunate reality in many schools. It doesn't have to stay that way. In schools that get it right, support becomes part of the design, not something reactive. A structure that helps educators respond before patterns become harder to change and needs escalate

That structure is called an MTSS.

At its core, MTSS is a way of organizing how schools respond to student needs. According to the Center on Multi-Tiered System of Supports (n.d.), MTSS is "a proactive and preventative framework that integrates data and instruction to maximize student achievement and support students' academic, behavioral, and social-emotional needs." It moves away from one-size-fits-all placements and toward a more flexible mindset. A way of saying, "Support should be flexible. And students shouldn't have to fail to get it."

In practice, MTSS organizes support into multiple levels, often called tiers. Tier 1 includes the instruction and support that all students receive. Tier 2 adds targeted help for students who need a little more, while Tier 3 offers more individualized support for students with more intensive needs. These tiers aren't fixed groups or boxes to place students in. They're meant to be flexible. A student might receive small-group reading support for six weeks and then return to core instruction. Another might need behavioral support during transitions but manage the rest of the day independently. The goal isn't to label students or track them permanently. It's to respond early, adjust often, and make sure support matches the need.

When MTSS works well, both students and teachers benefit. It gives them a shared process, a common language, and a clear pathway for what to try when something isn't working. Most importantly, it gives students access to support without requiring them to be removed from their classroom or labeled in order to get it.

At one elementary school, the fifth-grade team had been documenting repeated classroom disruptions from a student named Jeremiah. He was getting out of his seat constantly, making loud comments during lessons, and challenging directions almost daily. He wasn't aggressive, but the behavior was escalating. The kind of thing that made teachers start asking whether it was time to refer him for special education.

Instead, the team took a step back and used their MTSS process.

They reviewed notes from multiple classrooms and realized the pattern was clearest during transitions and unstructured time. Jeremiah wasn't struggling all day, only during certain parts of it. That was important. Instead of moving straight to a referral, they made a plan.

Jeremiah was added to a Tier 2 behavior support through the Check, Connect, and Expect program. He started each morning with a brief check-in, where a trained behavior coach reviewed his goals and gave him his daily progress card. Throughout the day, his teachers provided quick feedback tied to specific expectations like staying in his seat during instruction, using an inside voice, and following directions the first time. In the afternoon, he checked out with the coach, talked through how things went, and brought a copy of his progress home. The consistency gave him something to count on. This kind of structure has been shown to reduce problem behaviors and strengthen school engagement, particularly when implemented proactively as part of Tier 2 support (Cheney et al., 2009). Over time, his behavior became more predictable, his goals felt within reach, and his connection to school started to improve.

It didn't solve everything right away, but it was a clear step forward. Within a few weeks, the number of disruptions dropped. Jeremiah started using a signal when he needed a break instead of acting out. And the tone around him changed. Teachers stopped seeing him as "the problem." They saw a kid who responded to structure, consistency, and a bit more time to reset between tasks.

Because there was a system in place, no one had to go it alone. Jeremiah was able to receive support without needing a label first.

Making MTSS Work in Real Schools

Understanding the tiers is one thing. Making them work in a real school building is another.

You can have a beautiful diagram posted in the staff lounge and still have no system for who's doing the interventions, when they're happening, or how families are brought into the loop. This is where implementation breaks down. It's not that the model doesn't work; it's that the scaffolding hasn't been built to support it.

Equity within MTSS isn't only about who's on the list for support. It's about whether support is actually possible. Whether the school has created the conditions for it to happen in a consistent, timely, and respectful way.

MTSS belongs in general education. It isn't meant to be a workaround for special education. In many schools, though, the first instinct when a student struggles is still to "call in the specialist." It may be the default in some buildings, but it misses the point of MTSS entirely.

For the system to work, the entire team has to be part of it: general educators, special educators, interventionists, school counselors, administrators, paraprofessionals, and school psychologists. Each of them has a role to play, and not in isolation.

These are the people who notice the small changes in behavior and catch patterns early. They know what actually works for their students. When those insights are shared and coordinated, support becomes more than patchwork. It becomes how the school thinks

This doesn't require hiring a dozen new staff members. It means looking at the people already in the building and thinking intentionally about how their time is being used. Collaboration has to be part of the structure, not something teachers are left to find time for on their own.

Even the most well-designed intervention plan won't work if there's no time to deliver it.

In many schools, the hardest part isn't figuring out what students need. It's finding a time in the day to make it happen. Core instruction takes priority, and everything else gets squeezed in. That often means pulling students out and hoping they catch up on what they missed.

Leadership plays a critical role here. Schools that make MTSS work don't wait for an open window. They create time into their calendar so that teams can plan, review data, and adjust support. One school used its scheduled early release professional development days to carve out dedicated time for grade-level teams to meet. That time wasn't used for compliance tasks or catch-up grading. It was used to talk about students, plan interventions, and decide what needed to change for the week ahead.

Those small adjustments added up, and over time, the schedule started working for the support system instead of working against it.

When MTSS Becomes Culture

In too many schools, families only get called in when something has already gone sideways. By then, it often feels like the decision's already been made.

MTSS offers a different opportunity. One that brings families in from the beginning. When a student is struggling, the conversation includes what's already being done to help, what the school is noticing, and what families are seeing at home. They're not sitting on the outside of the process. They're part of it.

Novak and Rodriguez (2023) emphasize that equity within MTSS means making space for family voice, especially for students who have been historically underserved or misunderstood. That might mean using multiple ways to communicate, like phone calls, text messages, or in-person chats after school, so families don't have to rearrange their lives just to be heard. For multilingual families, it means communication in their home language. For working families, it might mean meetings outside the standard nine-to-five window or offering updates through whatever format is most accessible.

The point isn't to get everything right, it's to establish trust through genuine partnership. When families see that schools are paying attention early, and responding, they're more likely to lean in. That kind of trust changes everything.

MTSS works best when it becomes part of the school's everyday way of thinking. It isn't a form to fill out or a meeting to check off. It becomes the everyday way that adults in the building notice, respond, and adjust.

In schools where this mindset takes root, support doesn't feel like something extra. It feels expected. A student who's struggling isn't seen as a problem to fix or a case to open. A student who's struggling isn't immediately seen as a problem to fix or a case to open. They're seen as someone who needs something different for a little while, and the school already has a way to figure out what that is.

That's when the system starts to feel real. The system may not be perfect, but when it's responsive, it gives students what they need most.

Research Highlights: Why MTSS Matters

MTSS isn't a framework that looks good in theory but disappears in practice. When schools implement it with purpose and commit to early support, coordinated systems, and shared responsibility, it can change the trajectory for students.

A study from WestEd (Gage et al., 2024) tracked the impact of MTSS across three elementary schools that received direct coaching. The results were clear: students in those schools had significantly fewer behavior incidents than their peers in comparison schools. They were also much less likely to have even a single office referral.

The impact went beyond behavior. Those same schools saw noticeable gains in attendance. Over two years, students missed fewer days of school, suggesting that MTSS may be helping create environments students actually want to be part of.

The progress didn't come from a new curriculum or a set of flashy tools. It came from schools organizing themselves around a shared structure, using collaboration, data, and early support to respond before problems became patterns. These schools didn't separate academics from behavior. They treated student needs as connected and acted accordingly.

Other research backs this up. McIntosh and Goodman (2016) found that when MTSS is implemented with fidelity, schools see reduced discipline referrals and narrowed opportunity gaps, especially for students who have historically been underserved. Fuchs et al. (2012) showed that early intervention, particularly in reading, can significantly reduce the number of students later referred for special education services. And working conditions are important too. Harris et al. (2019) found that student behavior is one of the most influential factors shaping teacher perceptions of their work environment. A factor strongly tied to job satisfaction and attrition. When schools use MTSS to respond to behavioral needs early and consistently, they're not only supporting students. They're also creating conditions where educators are more likely to stay, because support is working for everyone, not only the few who need it most.

Catching Potential, Not Just Problems

At the core of early intervention is a commitment to seeing students clearly, before their challenges begin to define them. The goal isn't to avoid something. It's to design something better. A path where students aren't delayed in getting what they need. A system where help is available without layers of paperwork or long delays.

This begins with asking better questions. Not "How do I get this student through the day?" but "What do they need to feel successful here?" or "What might this moment be telling me?" These questions help shift our focus from reacting to behavior or academic gaps toward understanding what's actually going on beneath the surface. That shift in perspective can quietly change everything about how we respond.

Insight, however, isn't enough. It has to be matched with the structure. That's where MTSS comes in. Not as a formality, but as a usable framework. A system that creates space for early support and rests on shared responsibility. When schools are built to respond early and adapt in real time, students don't have to wait until things fall apart before they're seen.

That deserves attention, because when support only kicks in after a referral, we've already let too much time pass. Frustration has built, and students have spent valuable time sitting with the belief that school isn't for them. Even when support arrives, the feeling of being behind is hard to shake. It doesn't disappear with a small group or a new plan.

Early guardianship invites us to think differently. To design classrooms and systems that expect variation and respond to it. That see differences as part of learning, not disruptions from it. It reminds us that support shouldn't be saved for when something is broken. It can be part of the everyday.

The first step is noticing. Slowing down enough to see what's actually happening. From there, it's about collaboration. Teachers talk with each other, loop in specialists, and invite families into the process in ways that feel purposeful, not performative. When that happens, support stops being a scramble. It becomes part of how school works.

What students gain from that isn't only academic growth. They feel capable. They feel connected. They feel like they belong.

This kind of structure doesn't exist in isolation. It depends on teams that trust each other, share what they see, and work toward the same purpose. As we move into the next chapter, we shift from early support to shared effort. The power of MTSS, and the promise of early guardianship, comes from the alignment of people who are supported, connected, and ready to respond together.

The better question isn't who needs help. It's how we build a system that ensures no one has to wait for it.

References

Center on Multi-Tiered System of Supports. (n.d.). *Essential components of MTSS*. American Institutes for Research. https://mtss4success.org/essential-components

Cheney, D., Stage, S. A., Hawken, L. S., Lynass, L., Mielenz, C., & Waugh, M. (2009). A 2-year outcome study of the Check, Connect, and Expect intervention for students at risk for severe behavior problems. *Journal of Emotional and Behavioral Disorders, 17*(4), 226–243. https://doi.org/10.1177/1063426609339186

Fuchs, D., Fuchs, L. S., & Compton, D. L. (2012). Smart RTI: A next-generation approach to multilevel prevention. *Exceptional Children, 78*(3), 263–279. https://doi.org/10.1177/001440291207800301

Gage, N. A., Salomonson, K., Ballew, T., Clavenna-Deane, B., & Grasley-Boy, N. (2024). *The impact of multi-tiered systems of support (MTSS) on student attendance and behavior*. WestEd. https://www.wested.org/resource/impact-of-multi-tiered-systems-of-support-mtss-on-student-attendance-and-behavior/

Harris, S. P., Davies, R. S., Christensen, S. S., Hanks, J., & Bowles, B. (2019). Teacher attrition: Differences in stakeholder perceptions of teacher work conditions. *Education Sciences, 9*(4), 300. https://doi.org/10.3390/educsci9040300

McIntosh, K., & Goodman, S. (2016). *Integrated multi-tiered systems of support: Blending RTI and PBIS*. Guilford Press.

Novak, K., & Rodriguez, K. (2023). *In support of students: A leader's guide to equitable MTSS*. Jossey-Bass.

Radley, K. C., Fischer, A. J., Dubrow, P., Mathis, S. N., & Heller, H. (2024). Reducing teacher distress through implementation of the Good Behavior Game. *Journal of Behavioral Education*, *33*(4), 890–911. https://doi.org/10.1007/s10864-023-09515-7

7

Assembling the League
The Strength of Collaboration

A parent on an Individualized Education Program (IEP) support message board once shared how they'd stayed up all night rewriting the draft IEP they received. Not because they were trying to be difficult, but because the document didn't sound like their child at all. It was cold, clinical, and full of deficit language. Yes, they actually used the term deficit language. McClure and Reed (2022) argue the same point in *Hacking Deficit Thinking*: deficit-based language in education influences the way we see kids, and then impacts the way we support them. If the words focus only on problems, the plans do, too.

In this particular instance, their child was described with words like "abnormalities" and "delays." The kind of words that might be technically accurate but are still hard for a parent to read or hear about their child. By the time the parent hit "save" on their edits, they weren't just tired. They were angry and ready to go into the meeting and fight. Not physically, of course. But you could feel the emotional armor going on. You could hear the exhaustion behind the determination.

That story isn't rare. IEP meetings were never meant to be battlegrounds, but for a lot of families, that's exactly what they become. Parents swap advice like "Never go alone" or "Bring an advocate every time." And that level of distrust? It doesn't come out of nowhere. It's from years of not being heard, from plans that felt written for the system rather than the student, from teams that didn't feel like teams at all.

But special education isn't the superhero that swoops in to save the day. It never was. The real power happens when people come together. Educators, school psychologists, specialists, administrators, and families work side by side to design something stronger than any one person could create alone.

Systems and policies set the stage. The most meaningful change happens in the relationships between people. In the conversations and decisions that are made when there's no clear answer. The same way a teacher and a parent talk through options without needing to win, simply trying to get it right.

The hard truth is this: collaboration doesn't count only when it's easy. The real test is what happens when it's not. A disagreement that no one saw coming. When things are tense. A student whose needs don't fit neatly into a box or a program. That's when a team's strength actually counts.

Because the best teams don't only show up when the paperwork says so. They establish trust over time. They communicate regularly. They check in, adjust, and try again. They don't pretend to have all the answers. They really believe they'll get closer to the right one if they stay at the table together.

There's research to support this. Banerjee et al. (2017) found that student achievement, especially in reading, benefits when teachers report higher job satisfaction. Now here's the key: that satisfaction wasn't happening in isolation. It showed up most in schools with strong professional communities and a culture of teacher collaboration. The real work is showing up when things are uncomfortable: like answering the hard email, taking the call, or sitting in the meeting even when you're frustrated. That's what moves things forward. That's what builds trust.

We all remember, hopefully, those meetings that seem to work effortlessly. The ones where the conversation seems like a true conversation, not a presentation. Where everyone comes to the table, brings something, listens, says something, and leaves with a shared plan that makes sense. You step out of the room thinking, *That was good. That felt like we actually got some real work done.*

In many cases, it's the other kind of meeting we remember even better. The one that didn't go quite right. Maybe it started tense, or someone came in clearly upset. Maybe there were distractions or outside pressures. Sometimes the agenda falls apart, and no matter how prepared you were, the meeting veers into territory you didn't expect.

I've had meetings like that. We all have. Moments where it felt like people were speaking different languages. Where emotions ran high, or trust was already on shaky ground before the meeting even started.

One thing I pay the most attention to is this. A lot of the time, the tone of the meeting doesn't start in the meeting. It starts way before that. In the hallway conversations, in the emails that get answered quickly and respectfully, in the way you respond to concerns when there's no audience watching. I've spent years trying to establish strong, steady relationships with the people I work with. The families, advocates, attorneys, specialists, because by the time we sit down together, I want the foundation to already be there.

That's not to say it always works. It doesn't. I've had my fair share of hard meetings, emotional ones, meetings where nothing got resolved in that hour or more and the only real progress came later. However, I don't take it personally. Most parents are showing up to fight for what they believe their child needs. So am I. If we can start from that place, even if we don't see the path forward yet, there's a much better chance we'll eventually find it.

Maybe that's the place to start. Assume the person across the table is trying. School teams are stretched thin and still doing their best with the resources they have. Parents are doing everything they can with what they've been told and what they've seen in their own child. The important part is noticing the effort. It doesn't always show up clearly. Sometimes it's hard to read or easy to miss, but it's there. People show up in different ways, and that still counts.

Collaboration isn't only about what happens in the IEP room. It's about everything that leads up to it, and everything that follows after.

I once worked with a family where things started off strong. The initial evaluation went smoothly, the eligibility meeting felt solid, and the IEP team came together with a sense of real collaboration. People were asking thoughtful questions, tossing out ideas, and leaving with what felt like a shared plan. One of those meetings where you walk out thinking, *Okay, that went well.*

I don't know why, but something changed not long after.

No one ever said it directly, but the tone changed. Emails felt sharper. Meeting requests became more formal. There were long silences where there used to be quick replies. From the school's perspective, it felt like the family no longer trusted the team. From the family's perspective, it may have felt like the school had stopped listening. Whatever the cause, the relationship that had once felt easy now felt strained.

The difficult part? We couldn't fix it overnight. There was no single moment of resolution, no big turning point where everything got sorted out. The discomfort lingered. The tension showed up in meetings and phone calls for months. I won't pretend it was easy, as that tension lasted for years.

But we kept showing up. We stayed consistent. We responded even when the messages were hard to read. We kept inviting the family to the table, even when it was hard to read the room. Even when we weren't sure how things would be received. Because showing up, listening, and continuing to try is what the student needed. That's what they deserved.

Eventually, the tone softened. Conversations started to feel more collaborative again. The parent began joining meetings with fewer reservations. We weren't back to where we started, exactly, but we'd figured out how to work together again. This doesn't mean that everything got resolved, but we kept showing up and doing the work anyway.

That's the part of collaboration people don't always talk about. It's not always smooth. It's not always predictable. Sometimes things just go sideways, and sometimes there's not much you can do about it in the moment. You keep trying and keep showing up. You hope that over time, trust can be rebuilt, even if it looks different than it did before.

Because that's the work. It's not perfect relationships, nor always getting it right. It is doing the best you can to stay at the table.

Rewriting What It Means to Work Together

If you've been in education long enough, you've probably heard a lot of familiar language about collaboration, Professional Learning Community (PLC) meetings, co-teaching models, team teaching, and vertical alignment. We have talked about some of these topics already. It all sounds good on paper. Too often, "collaboration" gets reduced to a shared Google Drive folder or a quick check-in between meetings.

What John Hattie's research reminds us is that collaboration isn't simply a feel-good idea. Done right, it's one of the most powerful tools we have.

In *Visible Learning: The Sequel* (Hattie, 2023), Hattie zeroes in on Collective Teacher Efficacy (CTE) as one of the most significant predictors of student success. With an effect size of 1.34, it outpaces nearly every other intervention out there. That number isn't a mere statistic; it's a wake-up call. Because CTE isn't about individual teacher talent. It's about what happens when entire teams believe in their shared capacity to make a difference.

Let that sink in: the belief that we, as a team, can impact outcomes is more powerful than most instructional programs, curriculum changes, or tech tools.

Hattie doesn't stop at belief. He talks about pedagogically productive inquiry, which sounds a bit lofty, but at its core, it's about asking better questions together. The kind of questions that focus on what we're doing, why we're doing it, and whether it's actually helping students grow.

It's not collaboration if we're simply going through the motions or sharing updates. It's collaboration when we're willing to get into the hard stuff. To ask: Why is this student struggling with reading comprehension when they've mastered decoding? What did we try already, and how do we know it helped? Where did we see growth, and where did we miss something?

That kind of inquiry can be uncomfortable. Because it means getting direct. It means facing gaps in our practice or noticing when a strategy we've used for years might not be serving the students in front of us today.

It's also incredibly powerful. Because when we stop working in isolation and start examining our practices together, with intention, with evidence, and with humility, things begin to change.

What This Actually Looks Like in Schools

Let's ground this in something real.

Imagine a sixth-grade team meeting at the end of a long day. Everyone's tired. The math scores from the latest benchmark came in, and they're not great. It would be easy for people to tune out, blame external factors, or say "these kids just aren't ready for middle school."

Instead, the team leader starts with a different tone. "What do these scores actually tell us?" she asks. "More importantly, what do they not tell us yet?"

Then, something different happens. People start talking, and I mean really talking. They are not talking about curriculum pacing or mandates, but about student thinking. One teacher mentions how some students solved problems correctly but couldn't explain why. Another brings up a hands-on activity that seemed to finally make fractions click for a few kids. Someone pulls out student work samples and asks, "Are we missing a misconception here?"

That's pedagogically productive inquiry.

We don't always have to have the flashiest slides or the most put-together lesson plan. What can make a difference is the willingness to stay curious. To ask why something worked, or didn't, and what that tells us about how kids learn.

That's where the change happens. When the conversation moves beyond logistics and compliance and into something more intentional. When it stops being about who did what and starts becoming about what's actually helping students move forward.

From Collegiality to Real Collaboration

Too often, we mistake collegiality for collaboration. We assume that being friendly, sharing a few resources, or sitting on the same committee means we're working together. However, Hattie challenges us to push further.

Real collaboration isn't about keeping things smooth or conflict-free. It's about making time for the conversations that aren't easy. It's taking a real look at the data, even when it brings up things we'd rather not see. It's moving beyond polite agreement toward something more grounded: shared clarity, consistency, and a real sense of collective responsibility.

This part gets personal. Because the kind of collaboration Hattie is talking about only happens when there's trust. Not the "we get along fine" kind of trust, but the kind that lets people say, "I'm not sure," or "Maybe I got that wrong," without fear. If that safety's not there, the work stays shallow, careful, and polite.

Being polite doesn't move student learning forward.

In my own experience, the most meaningful progress doesn't happen when everyone agrees. It happens when we don't. When someone raises a concern I hadn't considered. When a teammate sees the same problem through a completely different lens. Those moments, while sometimes tough, are often the most productive because they push us to think in ways we might not have on our own.

The better question, then, isn't whether we're meeting as a team. It's whether our team is strong enough to wrestle with different ideas, stay in the conversation when it gets uncomfortable, and still walk out of the room focused on the same student.

The Role of Leadership in Building Collective Efficacy

Sometimes the difference between a team that functions and one that actually works well together comes down to leadership. It's not about having all the answers. It's about how leaders shape the day-to-day. The way they run meetings. The way they respond when something doesn't go as planned. The way they listen, or don't. You can feel it in the building. People speak up, or they stay quiet. Meetings move with purpose, or they drag. Trying something new either feels supported, or it feels risky.

When leaders stay curious, invite reflection, and make room for disagreement, something changes. Teams start to ask better questions. People talk through what didn't work and why. They begin to take risks, not because they have to, but because the space feels safe enough to try.

That's when collaboration starts to develop. It stops being about appearances and becomes real. People doing the work, with and for each other.

One study that backs this up comes from Sohail et al. (2023), who reviewed over a hundred studies on teacher well-being and burnout. Across all the data, one pattern was clear: teachers who felt supported by their leadership, both socially and professionally, were more likely to report strong well-being, greater job satisfaction, and a higher sense of instructional efficacy. That support showed up in steady, consistent ways: building trust, noticing effort, making sure people felt included, and creating room for real collaboration. When teachers felt better supported, their students did better too.

In other words, collective efficacy isn't something that happens in team meetings. It grows out of the everyday climate of the school. When a principal says, "I trust your judgment," and backs it up with action, it is significant. When an administrator asks how a new strategy is working instead of only checking if it's being done, it develops confidence. When leaders listen, and keep listening, teams take more ownership.

The reverse is just as true. When leadership avoids the hard conversations, pushes compliance over connection, or shuts down questions, then trust erodes. People disengage. They go through the motions, and collaboration becomes a performance instead of a practice.

So yes, leadership is important. Leaders help shape whether people feel like their voices are heard and their efforts mean something.

Common Pitfalls (and How to Avoid Them)

Even with the best intentions, collaboration can fall apart. The system makes it easy to slip into habits that leave little room for real thinking. We still call it collaboration, but too often it turns into something else.

> Pitfall #1: Mistaking compliance for teamwork
> Just because everyone is in the room doesn't mean they're working as a team. Sometimes meetings become about reporting out, sharing updates, reviewing plans, moving through the checklist. That kind of structure can feel efficient, but it leaves little room for curiosity or real dialogue. When collaboration turns into a routine instead of a process, no one walks away thinking differently than when they walked in.
>
> What helps: Provide opportunities for real conversation. Real collaboration isn't always neat. Some of the best conversations often start when someone breaks from the agenda and says, "Can we press pause and actually talk about this?" Normalize slowing down.
>
> Pitfall #2: Using data as a weapon
> Data are supposed to inform. But when they're used to prove a point, justify a decision, or call out individuals, they create fear. Teachers stop sharing. Families stop trusting. Instead of becoming a tool for understanding student needs, data become something people brace for.
>
> What helps: Focus on patterns, not people. Ask, "What are we seeing?" and "What might we be missing?" Use data to guide the work, not grade the people.
>
> Pitfall #3: Blame culture
> When things go wrong, it's easy to start pointing fingers. "Well, the teacher didn't follow through." "The parent didn't show up." "The student didn't try." We need to acknowledge that blame shuts down learning. It makes people defensive. It creates walls instead of solving problems.

What helps: Change the language. Instead of "Who dropped the ball?" ask "What made this fall through?" Assume good intentions. Most of the time, people aren't trying to avoid responsibility. They're trying to manage a lot with limited capacity.

Pitfall #4: Overlooking the quiet voices
Some people speak easily in groups, while others don't. That doesn't mean they don't have insight. When only the loudest voices get heard, we miss the nuance. We miss the people who might be holding the key to a better idea.

What helps: Make room for multiple ways to contribute. Ask people directly what they think. Circle back after the meeting. Pay attention to who's not speaking, and wonder why.

A 2024 study by Fleming, Calvert, and Turner found something that, frankly, makes sense: when educators felt like it was okay to speak up, make mistakes, and disagree without being shut down, everything worked better. Burnout was lower. Relationships were stronger. People felt more supported by their leadership. That sense of safety didn't erase the stress, especially during the chaos of the pandemic, but it gave people something steady to hold onto.

That's the real work in education. Not avoiding missteps, but catching them early. Naming them and creating habits that keep collaboration from becoming another word we use without really meaning it.

Everyday Moves That Build Strong Teams

Strong teams don't form all at once. They grow through small, consistent moments. The hallway conversations. The way someone shows up to a meeting. The tone of a follow-up email. A quick check-in in the hallway. These aren't the things that get written up in official plans, but they shape how people feel about working together. Over time, they make a bigger difference than we tend to admit.

These small moves cannot be looked over. And while they're not complicated, they do take intention.

1. **Start with curiosity**
    Before jumping in with solutions, pause and ask a real question. A question that actually gives the other person a moment to talk about what they're noticing. Try something like, "What's your take on this?" works. So does "What have you been seeing with this student?" A thoughtful simple question can change the tone of the whole conversation.
2. **Give people the benefit of the doubt**
    It's easy to assume someone dropped the ball. However, most of the time, there's more to the story. Collaboration falls apart when we assume the worst. It gets much stronger when we believe that most people are genuinely doing the best they can with what they have. That kind of thinking cultivates a setting for grace, and that context makes the work more sustainable.
3. **Follow up**
    When someone brings up a concern or shares something vulnerable, follow up. A short email. A quick check-in. Even saying, "I've been thinking about what you shared." It shows you were listening. That creates trust.
4. **Name what's working**
    It's easy to get stuck in problem-solving mode, especially in special education. But strong teams take time to notice progress. Call out when something clicked. Celebrate small wins. Let people know their work deserves attention.
5. **Make room in the conversation**
    If you've already noticed that some people tend to stay quiet, don't just hope that changes. Create a pathway where it can. That might mean following up after the meeting, making time in the moment, or asking someone directly, "What do you think?" Sometimes it's not that people don't have ideas. They haven't been given a real opening to share them.

6. **Keep the student at the center**
   When the conversation starts to drift toward policy, paperwork, or preferences, bring it back: "What does this student need right now?" That question has a way of cutting through the noise and refocusing the team on what actually is important.

None of these things are revolutionary. They're the kind of small, repeated choices that make a team feel like a team. The more consistent they become, the easier it is to face the hard stuff together.

Collaboration Across Lines

The strongest teams aren't made up of only people in the same department or grade level. They form across roles: teachers, specialists, paraprofessionals, counselors, school psychs, admin, and families. If someone's part of that student's day, they're part of the team. Whether their name's on the IEP or not.

That kind of collaboration doesn't simply happen. Too often, support staff are left out of planning conversations. Sometimes families are technically present but not truly included. They get updates instead of invitations to problem-solve. Even within the school building, people end up working in silos. They're well-intentioned, but disconnected. When that happens, students get mixed messages. Expectations move further away. Communication breaks down. Support starts to feel fragmented.

That same 2023 review by Sohail and colleagues also found that inclusive environments, where every team member feels valued and included, are directly tied to stronger perceptions of school climate, collaboration, and overall job satisfaction. When paraprofessionals, specialists, and families are treated as full participants, not afterthoughts, teams function better and students benefit.

Because no single person ever has the full picture. A paraprofessional might notice something a teacher missed. A parent might share something that reshapes how we understand a student's behavior. A counselor might catch a pattern before it shows up in academics. When those insights are shared, and actually heard, everyone gets a clearer view of what's going on and what the student needs. Leonard and Woodland (2022) found that when teachers engaged in meaningful, student-facing collaboration, they were more likely to use strategies that directly supported social-emotional learning. I would say, that's not accidental. It's a sign that when teams work together with intention, students feel it, not only in how they're supported, but in how they're taught.

That only happens when we reinforce systems that make it possible. It starts by asking, "Who else should be part of this?" Every voice at the table deserves real respect, no matter the title. What is worth noting is what each person sees and brings. Families should feel like partners in the work, not like outsiders looking in.

Collaboration works best when everyone at the table has a real role. That includes more than the people with titles or the ones who talk the most.

When It's Not Working

Not every meeting feels like a team coming together. You might be sitting there, listening to people talk, trying to figure out what's off. Everyone's present, and you are moving through the agenda, yet something's missing. The conversation doesn't go anywhere. The room feels flat.

People bring frustration with them, exhaustion, or tension that's been building for a while. In some cases, trust is already worn down before anyone even sits at the table.

It's easy to pull back in those moments. To do what's required, say what needs to be said, and leave it at that. But that's often when it counts the most to stay in it.

There's no quick fix. Most of the time, there isn't even a clear answer. What is imperative is how people respond in the hard moments. The moments where it can be uncomfortable, or no one really speaks. That's what defines the team. It tells people whether this is a place where we can keep working through things or whether we're on our own.

I've been in meetings where people really listened to each other. Where we didn't all agree, but we stayed in the conversation long enough to figure something out. I've also been in meetings where you could feel the tension as soon as you sat down. Where everyone was guarded. Where it felt like we were just trying to get through it.

What I've learned is this: the conditions are never perfect. You don't wait for the right team, the right mood, or the clean agenda. You keep showing up.

Maybe it's stepping back because your voice doesn't need to be the loudest one in the room that day.

Maybe it's staying in a conversation that feels complicated or stuck, not because you know exactly what to say, but because walking away won't help either.

Collaboration doesn't grow out of the easy moments. It takes shape when things are complicated, the path forward isn't clear, and people keep showing up anyway.

Students notice. They watch how the adults around them show up, especially when things are hard. When we keep showing up for each other, that kind of consistency becomes one of the strongest supports we can offer.

It's not about getting it right all the time.

It's about staying committed to the work and finding a way forward together.

References

Banerjee, N., Stearns, E., Moller, S., & Mickelson, R. A. (2017). Teacher job satisfaction and student achievement: The roles of teacher professional community and teacher collaboration in schools. *American Journal of Education, 123*(2), 203–241. https://doi.org/10.1086/689932

Fleming, C. M., Calvert, H. G., & Turner, L. (2024). Psychological safety among K–12 educators: Patterns over time, and associations with staff well-being and organizational context. *Psychology in the Schools, 61*(10), 2315–2337. https://doi.org/10.1002/pits.23165

Hattie, J. (2023). *Visible learning: The sequel*. Routledge.
Leonard, A., & Woodland, R. (2022). Teacher collaboration and instruction for social-emotional learning: A correlational study. *Current Issues in Education, 23*(3). https://doi.org/10.14507/cie.vol23iss3.2053
McClure, B., & Reed, K. (2022). *Hacking deficit thinking: 8 reframes that will change the way you think about strength-based practices and equity in schools*. Times 10 Publications.
Sohail, M. M., Baghdady, A., Choi, J., Huynh, H. V., Whetton, K., & Proeschold-Bell, R. J. (2023). Factors influencing teacher wellbeing and burnout in schools: A scoping review. *Work, 76*(5), 1317–1331. https://doi.org/10.3233/WOR-220234

8

Lifting the Signal
From Advocacy to Action

Most of us didn't sign up to work in education thinking we'd become activists. We may have imagined lesson plans and lightbulb moments, but probably not policy battles or data dives. If we care about kids, and I mean all kids, then we're already in the business of advocacy. We might not be calling it that.

And that means more than we might realize. Because every time we sit quietly while a student is placed in a segregated setting without challenge, every time we watch a colleague mislabel a child without questioning the process, every time we think, "Well, that's just how it is," we miss a chance to be the hero in someone's story.

As we have discussed, these are not the kind of heroes with catchphrases and blockbuster franchises. This is about the everyday kind. The ones who show up, ask hard questions, and stay in the room when the conversation gets uncomfortable. Real people, like you, who decide that they're not going to accept systems that underserve and overlook. It's about making moves that aren't always dramatic, but always deliberate. Moves that help change the narrative. From compliant educator or well-meaning parent to unapologetic advocate. From watching the storm to changing the weather.

So let's talk about how. But first, let's talk about why.

Setting the Stage: Why Advocacy Is More Important Now Than Ever

If you've ever second-guessed speaking up because you weren't sure it was your role, you're not alone. The system encourages it. Play nice. Don't rock the boat. Let the "experts" handle it. But the truth is, the boat is already full of holes, and staying quiet doesn't make you noble. It makes you complicit.

Every day, our students face inequities that are quietly embedded into the routines of school life. They aren't always flashy or headline-grabbing. They look like a school that offers Algebra I to eighth graders in some neighborhoods but not others. Like students of color disproportionately disciplined or denied access to advanced coursework. Like a child with a disability who gets sent home because the school "simply isn't equipped." These are the quiet injustices that need loud responses.

The 2021–22 Civil Rights Data Collection paints a picture that should stop us in our tracks (U.S. Department of Education, Office for Civil Rights, 2025). Despite decades of reform, disparities remain disturbingly consistent:

Students with disabilities make up only 14% of the school population. And yet, they make up nearly three out of every four students who are physically restrained at school.

Black students are 15% of the student body, but they make up a third of school-related arrests. A third. That's not a discipline problem. That's a system problem.

In high schools where most students are Black or Latino, only about one in three offers calculus. In mostly white schools? More than half do. That kind of access, or lack of it, shapes futures.

More than 2 million students attend schools with a police presence but no school counselor, and the majority of these students are Black or Latino.

Let that sink in.

These numbers raise hard questions. What do they say about who we invest in? Who we believe in? And who we quietly let fall through the cracks?

There's another truth worth naming. These patterns are not immovable. They are sustained by inertia. And they can be disrupted by people. Ordinary people. People like Sarah, the middle school teacher trying to meet every student's needs without losing herself. People like the parent who walks into an Individualized Education Program (IEP) meeting unsure, nervous, but unwilling to be sidelined. People who realize that silence is its own kind of endorsement.

This moment demands more than good intentions. It demands action. And that action doesn't have to be grand. It only has to be intentional. Colin Seale (2022) reminds us that equity can't stay an idea on a poster. It has to be something you can see, measure, and sustain. Otherwise, patterns stay the same.

So take a moment. Who is in your classroom, or your school, and isn't getting what they need? And what might change if you chose to do one thing differently?

That might look like reviewing your school's data with a thoughtful lens. Or advocating for stronger inclusive practices in your team meetings. Or noticing which students are always pulled out, always left out, and starting a conversation. Not with blame, but with purpose.

When many people hear the word advocacy, it likely invokes the image of lawyers or politicians. The truth is, that it is for us. It's for every educator who has ever said, "This isn't right." For every parent who's felt shut out of a conversation about their own child. For every school leader who's brave enough to ask, "Who is this system working for, and who is it failing?"

Advocacy doesn't have to be big or public. It often starts with noticing that something isn't right, and choosing not to ignore it. It's less about having the perfect solution and more about being willing to ask the harder, better questions.

So ask them. When the moment feels right. Or when it doesn't. But ask.

Because if we don't advocate for students, especially those most vulnerable, then who will?

The Many Faces of Advocacy

Advocacy doesn't belong to one role. It lives in the questions we ask, the choices we make, and the things we refuse to ignore. This is whether we're teachers, parents, administrators, or students themselves.

This is what often happens: people imagine advocacy as something other people do. The principal. The seasoned parent. The outside consultant. Someone more prepared, more connected, more confident. And because of that, too many educators and families talk themselves out of stepping in.

The truth is, advocacy wears a hundred faces. And most of them look like regular people trying to make something better in the spaces they already occupy.

Educators: Advocating from Inside the System

For educators, advocacy often begins in the small moments. Like noticing a pattern in referrals that raises a red flag. Or asking why a student was placed in a more restrictive setting again. Taking a second look at a behavior plan that seems more focused on meeting the basic requirements than actually supporting the student.

Sometimes it's what you say in a team meeting. Other times it's a conversation in the hallway, or a decision to follow up with a family that's been sidelined. It might be pushing your team to think differently about how progress is measured, or asking, "Is this really what's best for the student?"

It doesn't require a title. It takes a little courage to step into the conversation instead of stepping back. You need a listening ear and the patience to stay with it, even when it gets uncomfortable.

Parents: Experts in Their Child and the System

For parents, advocacy often begins at the kitchen table. In reading the procedural safeguards, preparing for an IEP meeting, or asking another parent for advice. It's often done without fanfare, squeezed in between work, caretaking, and everything else life demands. But it can be so impactful. And when parents feel equipped and supported, that advocacy can ripple far beyond their own families.

In one study, researchers worked with 37 parents of children with disabilities, offering a short legislative advocacy training that focused on special education law, IDEA reauthorization, and how to take action. After only a few hours of training, those parents left with more information and a clearer sense of what they could do next. They reached over 300 people through their advocacy, educating other parents, contacting legislators, and raising awareness in their communities (Burke et al., 2022).

Truth be told, this wasn't a massive program or a national campaign. It was a handful of parents choosing to act. And that choice made an impact.

The study also reminded us that knowledge gaps are real, and that they can get in the way. Even though IDEA is built around parent involvement, most of its legal language is hard to read and even harder to understand. In fact, some documents are written at a college reading level. So when parents feel overwhelmed or unsure, it's not because they aren't smart or invested. It's because we've made the rules nearly impossible to navigate.

That's why advocacy work has to include access. Information. Relationships. Opportunities to ask questions without being dismissed.

And yes, not every parent feels ready to talk to a legislator. But the study showed that telling another parent about IDEA reauthorization was the most common form of advocacy. Sharing what you know is a form of advocacy. So is joining a school committee. So is asking for something different on your child's IEP and explaining why.

It doesn't have to start big, but it does have to start.

Students: Learning to Speak for Themselves

We also can't talk about advocacy without naming students themselves. Too often, we talk around them, about them, or for them, but not with them. Self-advocacy is a skill, and it can be taught. Recently I was in a meeting with a middle school girl. We were discussing her IEP, and I was so impressed with her understanding of her needs and what she believed helped her navigate school. She talked about ELA and how that was an area that didn't come easily to her. She mentioned needing extra time to process verbal directions, and how noise sometimes made her feel overwhelmed or anxious. For a moment, she took over the meeting. No one interrupted her. I caught myself smiling. You could tell she'd been in so many of these meetings, and she was done performing. She was simply being honest.

And that's the thing. When kids speak, it doesn't need to be rehearsed or polished. They may need chances to practice. But even without perfect words, their voice carries weight. They need adults who believe they're capable of knowing what works for them.

And when we start giving them space to speak up in the small ways, they begin to see themselves as part of the process, not simply the subject of it.

Advocacy doesn't have to mean leading a meeting or pushing back on a decision. Sometimes it's as simple as asking a teacher for another way to show what they've learned. Or telling someone they're struggling, before it turns into a meltdown or a suspension.

When we make time for students to speak, we learn things we wouldn't have known otherwise. And when we actually listen, we're not only gathering information. We're sending a message: your voice counts here.

Elevating Educator Voice

We can't talk about meaningful change in education without listening to the people doing the work. And by "listening," I don't mean offering up a post-it wall at a PD day. I mean real voice. Real influence. Real partnership.

When educators are shut out of decision-making, when curriculum comes top-down without room to adapt, when mandates arrive without context or support, burnout isn't just likely, it's inevitable. And right now, teachers are burning out at alarming rates. That's not an exaggeration. A national survey found that nearly half of all teachers were planning to leave the profession within the next two years. Not because they don't care. Because the system doesn't always listen when they do (Ha et al., 2025).

But there's something else in the data, too. Something more hopeful. The same study found that autonomy holds value. Teachers who felt they had a say in how they teach, assess, and respond to student needs reported higher job satisfaction and lower burnout. Now it wasn't only about experience. Autonomy had a protective effect for teachers at all stages of their careers. It helped buffer the weight of high demands.

This lines up with what many of us already know from experience. When teachers feel trusted, supported, and seen as professionals, they're more likely to stay. They're more likely to speak up when something isn't working, and more likely to bring forward ideas that do.

And those ideas are important. Because educators are doing more than implementing systems. They're living in them. Every day. They know where things break down, and where they could be rebuilt better.

That's why we cannot afford to treat teacher voice as a luxury. It's a lever. A practical, necessary lever for school improvement. And if we want to shift the outcomes for students, especially those who've been underserved, we have to start by asking: What are our teachers seeing that we're not?

This is where advocacy and autonomy meet. Because when teachers are given space to ask hard questions, to shape the decisions that impact their students, to say "this doesn't work" without fear. They become some of our most powerful change agents.

It can't fall only on individual courage. School leaders and policymakers have a role to play here. They need to create systems that help educators use their voices instead of making it harder. That might mean carving out real time for collaboration. Or rethinking professional learning so it actually supports the work, instead of adding one more thing to the list. It might mean pausing long enough to ask teachers what support actually looks like before launching a new initiative.

We don't need more top-down fixes. We need more inside-out solutions.

And that starts by recognizing that teacher voice isn't something to "invite." It's something to build around.

Reimagining Advocacy Through an Intersectional Lens

If we want to advocate effectively, we have to be willing to see the whole child, not only the label on their paperwork. And that means understanding how disability, race, language, gender, and class come together in ways that shape students' lives in and out of school.

Too often, disability is treated like a single-issue concern. It's pulled out of conversations about race, equity, and justice, as if it lives in a separate category. But that separation isn't real. It's a product of systems that divide, rank, and sort. And when we don't name how those systems work together, we miss the full picture.

A powerful framework called Disability-Centered Culturally Sustaining Pedagogies (Kulkarni et al., 2024) pushes us to think differently. It reminds us that disabled youth of color don't just experience racism or ableism. They live at the intersection of both, and often much more. And they're not broken. They're navigating a system that was never built for them in the first place.

This framework doesn't diagnose the problem. It offers a path forward. One grounded in the lived knowledge of disabled activists, poverty scholars, and community organizers. People who have spent years not only surviving the system, but pushing back against it and creating something better.

One of the most important shifts the authors call for is this: stop framing disability as a deficit. Start recognizing it as an identity. A source of perspective. A part of a person's cultural and lived experience. When we hold that lens, it's a reminder that students aren't the problem. The barriers around them are. And we have more control over those than we sometimes admit.

That changes how we teach. It changes how we plan. It changes who we see as experts.

It also means being honest about the ways schools send messages. Sometimes subtly, sometimes not. Messages about who belongs and who doesn't. About what's considered "normal" and what isn't. The article shares that many teacher candidates, especially those of color, enter the field already carrying their own experiences of being overlooked or misunderstood in school. Those memories stay with them. And they can shape how they show up for students who are experiencing the same thing now.

When we start to understand these intersections, advocacy looks different. It's not merely about accommodations. It's about dismantling the conditions that made them necessary in the first place. It's about expanding what counts as knowledge, whose voices are seen as valid, and what kinds of learning environments actually honor the full humanity of every student.

This work is hard. It means unlearning a lot of what we've been taught about what "good" teaching looks like. But it also opens up something powerful. Possibility. The possibility of classrooms that aren't only inclusive in theory, but liberating in practice.

Advocacy in Action: Real Stories from the Field

Advocacy doesn't always show up with a sign or a speech. Sometimes it looks like a seemingly small moment that turns into a turning point. What is important isn't the size of the action. It's the intention behind it.

Here are a few stories that show what advocacy can look like in real schools, with real people, doing what they can from where they are.

1. **A General Educator Pushes Back on a Pattern**
   Melissa teaches fifth grade in a school where students with IEPs were almost always placed with the same teacher. That teacher was known for being "structured," and admin said it made scheduling easier. But Melissa started to notice something. The class lists weren't balanced.

Her colleague was overloaded. And more importantly, the students were being clustered in a way that felt more about convenience than support.

Melissa brought it up during a team meeting. At first, there was some defensiveness. "It's always been done this way." But she persisted. She asked if they could look at student needs alongside teacher strengths. She offered to co-plan with a special educator so she could take on more diverse learners herself. In truth, it wasn't a major policy change, but the next year's rosters looked different. More balanced. More thoughtful. The kind of shift that comes from noticing, and naming what others overlook.

2. **A Parent Who Knew Something Was Off**
Tariq's mom had been attending IEP meetings for years, but she always left with the feeling that something wasn't quite right. Her son was smart, funny, and curious, but all she kept hearing about were behavior issues. At one meeting, the team proposed a separate setting for "more support."

Instead of agreeing, she asked for the data that supported the decision. When it didn't add up, she requested an independent educational evaluation. Unfortunately, she felt the need and eventually brought in an advocate. She stayed steady, even when the room got tense.

Eventually, Tariq got the supports he needed, without being removed from his general education classroom. And his mom? She ended up helping three other families navigate similar situations that same year. Sometimes advocacy starts with your own child. Sometimes it doesn't end there.

3. **A High School Student Redefines Participation**
Janelle was a junior with an IEP. One of her underlying disabilities was ADHD, even if her IEP didn't explicitly state that. She definitely struggled with areas of executive functioning. Group projects were a nightmare.

It wasn't that she didn't care. She never quite knew where to start or how to keep all the moving pieces straight. Deadlines would sneak up. Group texts would overwhelm her. And when she fell behind, she shut down. Teachers assumed she was disengaged. Her peers did most of the work.

Eventually, one of her teachers pulled her aside. They talked through what was hard and what helped. Together, they came up with a plan: Janelle would take on specific roles she could manage, like designing slides or proofreading. Her teachers would check in with her earlier, not only after things started slipping.

It wasn't perfect. But it gave her a way in. And over time, she started to speak up more for herself. She began asking for reminders, clarifying deadlines, even suggesting alternate ways to participate. One small shift led to another. That's how systems start to move.

Call to Action: Becoming the Hero Your Students Need

You don't need a new title or a bigger platform to make a difference. You don't need to be the most experienced person in the room. You simply need to be willing to pay attention, and to act when the time is right.

That's what advocacy looks like most of the time. It's not flashy. It's not something that earns applause. But it's steady. It's noticing what no one else is talking about. It's circling back to a decision that didn't feel right. It's deciding that you're not going to wait for someone else to bring it up.

We've talked a lot about the systems that aren't working. But every broken system includes people who are willing to speak up. And that's where change begins.

Sometimes it's a conversation that happens after the meeting ends. Sometimes it's how you write your progress notes. Sometimes it's saying, "Can we slow down a minute? I want to make sure we're not missing something."

If you're reading this chapter, you've likely already felt that tug. That moment where your gut tells you to push back or ask a better question. The question is: What are you going to do with that?

This isn't about trying to do everything. It's about doing something. Starting somewhere.

Maybe it's this:

One policy you'll question. Maybe it's the way referrals are handled. Maybe it's how behavior data is used. Maybe it's how we define "success." Pick one and start asking why it exists, and who it really serves.

One student whose story you'll reframe. Not only on paper, but in how you talk about them, advocate for them, or challenge the assumptions being made around them.

One team meeting where you'll speak up. Not to be right. But to be honest. Maybe it's a question. Maybe it's a pause. Either way, it can make a difference.

You might be the only one at the table willing to speak up. But that doesn't mean you're alone.

Because this much is true: every time someone has pushed this work forward, it started with a moment like this one. A moment of choosing to see more. To say more. To expect more.

There are students in your school right now who have already decided how much they matter, based on how the adults around them treat their needs. Some of them have learned to be quiet. To go along. To expect less.

You can interrupt that. Not with some grand speech. Not with a perfect plan. But with how you show up. How you speak about kids when they're not in the room. How you advocate for families who feel like they're not being heard. How you choose not to ignore the tension when something doesn't feel right.

That's the work of a hero. Not the kind who saves the day in dramatic fashion. The kind who shows up again and again, choosing to care out loud. Choosing to pay attention. Choosing to believe that what we do in classrooms, in meetings, in passing conversations, it is essential.

And here's what matters most: someone is watching how you move through this work. A colleague. A parent. A student. You are teaching others what it looks like to stand up without walking out. To ask hard questions without giving up. To stay in the room and stay in the work.

So if you're looking for a sign? This is it.
Start there.

References

Burke, M. M., Rossetti, Z., & Li, C. (2022). The efficacy and impact of a special education legislative advocacy program among parents of children with disabilities. *Journal of Autism and Developmental Disorders*, *52*, 3271–3279. https://doi.org/10.1007/s10803-021-05258-4

Ha, C., Pressley, T., & Marshall, D. T. (2025). Teacher voices matter: The role of teacher autonomy in enhancing job satisfaction and mitigating burnout. *PLOS One*, *20*(1), e0317471. https://doi.org/10.1371/journal.pone.0317471

Kulkarni, S. S., Miller, A. L., Nusbaum, E. A., Pearson, H., & Brown, L. X. Z. (2024). Toward disability-centered, culturally sustaining pedagogies in teacher education. *Critical Studies in Education*, *65*(2), 107–127. https://doi.org/10.1080/17508487.2023.2234952

Seale, C. (2022). *Tangible equity: A guide for leveraging student identity, culture, and power to unlock excellence in and beyond the classroom*. Routledge.

U.S. Department of Education, Office for Civil Rights. (2025). *2021–22 Civil Rights Data Collection: A first look—Students' access to educational opportunities in U.S. public schools*. https://ocrdata.ed.gov

9

Beyond the Origin Story
Sustaining Change and Scaling Impact

Every superhero has an origin story. A defining moment. A call to action. Maybe it started with frustration like watching one too many students get pulled from class for services that didn't serve. Or maybe it was a single student who made you rethink everything. However, it began, something clicked. You decided to do something differently. To stop waiting for someone else to fix the system. You made your move.

Then what happens next?

That's the part they leave out of the origin story. The part after the cape comes off. After the Instagram post. After the PD session where everyone nodded along, and then Monday morning rolled around and nothing changed.

Because there is a part they don't show: real change isn't a montage. It's not set to inspiring music or wrapped up in three bullet points. It's slow. It's awkward. It's one step forward, two emails from district leadership, and a hallway conversation that makes you question whether you're the only one who still believes this is worth doing.

The education world is full of brave beginnings. Pilot programs with shiny binders. New inclusion models tested in a single grade level. Equity initiatives that start strong and quietly fade into the background noise of school improvement plans.

Too often, what begins as a bold step forward ends up siloed in one classroom, or tied to one person, or buried under the next round of state mandates.

The issue isn't a lack of care because there's plenty of that. It's that the system is wired to protect what's already in place, not to push for what could be better. The moment something starts to work, really work, it gets absorbed back into the same structures that created the problem in the first place.

Now this is where this chapter shifts the storyline. We're not here to romanticize the start. We're here to ask what it takes to keep going. Not only you, but your team. Your school. Your district. What would it take for inclusive, student-centered practices to stop being the exception and start being the expectation?

This isn't the end of the story. It's the part where the hero builds a team, changes the rules, and makes sure the next chapter doesn't look like the last. Let's talk about what it takes to make change stick.

From Pockets of Promise to Systems of Sustainability

If you spend enough time in schools, you start to see patterns. In almost every building, there's a classroom that feels like it's ahead of the curve. Students are engaged. Routines make sense. The teacher knows exactly when to offer support and when to step back. Kids with Individualized Education Programs (IEPs) aren't only physically present; they're part of what's happening. You see creative groupings, real differentiation, maybe even a few students who normally struggle leading the charge in a group discussion.

It works. Then you walk a few doors down and see the opposite. Same school. Same district. Completely different experience.

If you know what I am talking about then you know that this isn't unusual. If anything, it's the norm. We've built systems where great teaching and inclusive practices often depend on the right person in the right room at the right time. The problem isn't that good things aren't happening. The problem is they're not happening everywhere.

Promising practices tend to live in pockets. We tend to have pilot programs, "model" classrooms, specific grade levels, or schools that got a grant and managed to make it stretch. When those pockets aren't supported by broader systems, they stall. Or fade. Or quietly go back to business as usual the moment a schedule changes, a principal leaves, or test scores dip.

There are reasons for that. Structural ones. Like rigid master schedules that leave no time for planning across teams. Funding streams that separate special education dollars from general education ones, even when the work overlaps. PD that's one-size-fits-all, or worse, misaligned with what's actually happening in classrooms. There's cultural resistance, too. The sense that "this is how we've always done it," even if how we've always done it hasn't worked.

Add to that the narrative we keep reinforcing that what makes a school inclusive is one passionate teacher who's willing to go above and beyond. It sounds inspiring, but it's not a real strategy. It's not how you cultivate a sustainable model. Passion is important, sure. No one should have to burn themselves out just to make sure students with disabilities have access to what they need.

What they need isn't a mystery. The Supreme Court made that clear in *Endrew F.* when it said that students receiving special education services are entitled to more than minimal progress. They're entitled to an education that is "appropriately ambitious in light of their circumstances (Endrew F. v. Douglas County School District, 2017)." We talked about this earlier in the book, and it's worth repeating here: that bar is more than a legal requirement. It's a statement about value. About how much we believe a student is capable of when the system actually supports them.

Which brings us to equity. The National Equity Project (NEP) defines educational equity as each child receiving *what they need* to develop to their full academic and social potential (National Equity Project, 2016). It's a definition that goes far beyond access. Getting what you need in school should reflect who you are, how you learn, and the circumstances you bring with you each day.

Equity means education isn't one-size-fits-all. It's responsive, intentional, and built around real human differences.

For special education, this should be the guiding principle. However, too often, we fall back on compliance checklists and outdated models that assume "fair" means "equal." We create programs around what's convenient for adults instead of what's responsive to students. And we act surprised when gaps don't close.

The definition also asks us to go deeper. To "remove the predictability of success or failure based on social or cultural factors (NEP, 2016)" that includes disability. It includes race, language, socioeconomic status, and any combination of the above. When we look at who is consistently excluded, who is being sent out of class, or who is never part of enrichment opportunities, we're not looking at student deficits. We're looking at system design.

This is the part where intention has to meet infrastructure. If we really believe every student has unique strengths, then the way we run schools has to reflect that. It can't only be about good intentions or individual effort. We need to establish systems where those strengths actually have space to show up. That starts with a shared foundation, clear values, consistent practices, and expectations that don't shift depending on which classroom a kid walks into. Teachers will always bring their own approach and personality, but the core should stay solid.

We cannot keep designing systems where excellence is the exception. If inclusive practice depends on who your teacher is, it's not really inclusion. It's chance, and our students deserve more than that.

The Pillars of Sustainable Change

If inclusive education is going to stick, it has to be more than philosophy. It has to live in the day-to-day work of schools. It has to be in the policies we write, the leadership we follow, and the partnerships we reinforce. Otherwise, it risks becoming one more initiative that flares up and fades out. Real sustainability depends on doing the hard, unglamorous work of embedding these values into the actual structure of the system. Here are three places to start.

    a. **Policy That Doesn't Simply Sit on a Shelf**
Most schools don't need another vision statement. What they need is alignment between what they say they believe and what they actually do. That means inclusive values have to show up in the places that shape daily practice. In the school improvement plans, IEP protocols, hiring practices, and district-level guidance documents. Not buried in the introduction. Not tacked on at the end. Embedded.

        Let's take IEPs, for example. If we believe inclusion isn't only a placement but a mindset, then that has to show up in how we write goals and how we define access to the general education curriculum. IEPs should reflect a student's strengths and set ambitious, meaningful targets. Planning with that kind of purpose means getting clear about the student. What motivates them, how they learn, and where they can grow when the right support is in place. Lowering expectations or settling for vague goals doesn't serve anyone. Again something the *Endrew F.* decision explicitly reinforced (Endrew F. v. Douglas County School District, 2017).

        We also need policies that hold leaders accountable for how they staff and structure their schools. If a district claims to value inclusive education but continues to hire without looking for candidates with co-teaching experience, or refuses to schedule collaborative planning time, then that value is no more than words. Policy should drive hiring decisions, staff training, and even how schools allocate discretionary funds.

        Within classrooms, we can't keep treating differentiated instruction like an optional skill or a PD day buzzword. Carol Tomlinson's work has been clear about this for decades: differentiation isn't about making things easier or doing twelve versions of the same lesson. It's about recognizing varied readiness levels, interests, and learning profiles, and designing instruction that adapts accordingly (Tomlinson & Moon, 2013). That mindset should be a standard expectation across grade levels, not a nice-to-have.

Sustainable change starts when policy doesn't only describe inclusive practice. It requires it.

b. **Leadership That Models, Not Mandates**

When school leaders walk the talk, things change. You know what that looks like. They're in classrooms, not only in front offices. They ask questions that are meaningful. They know students by name. They don't hand out mandates. They model what deserves attention.

If leaders want to see inclusive, student-centered practices flourish, they have to engage with them directly. That means showing up in co-taught classrooms. Participating in team meetings. Asking how policies are landing in real time. Too often, leadership is positioned as distant and managerial when it needs to be instructional and collaborative.

We don't need one more meeting about tiered supports if no one can explain what they actually look like in action. And we certainly don't need principals evaluating teachers on inclusive practice when they've never seen it done well themselves.

Principals matter. A lot. When it comes to supporting students with disabilities, leadership plays a direct role in what inclusion actually looks like. Crockett (2002) found that schools are more likely to establish and sustain inclusive environments when principals prioritize things like collaboration, instructional support, and a clear, shared vision for equity. When leaders invest in inclusive scheduling, support co-teaching partnerships, and protect time for professional learning, those actions ripple across the building. What gets attention gets replicated. If a principal spends all their energy managing logistics and none observing inclusive classrooms or asking about IEP implementation, that sends a message about what is worth noting, and what isn't.

Leadership shows up in how time is spent and what gets prioritized. The choices leaders make, where they are, what they ask about, what they follow up on, send a clear message about what is important in a school. If you want to create a culture where inclusion is non-negotiable, then you have to lead from inside it.

c. **Community as Co-Creators**

Sustainable change doesn't happen in isolation. It also doesn't stick simply because a district rolls out a new plan. For inclusive education to take root, communities need to be involved from the start. Not only consulted after the fact, but brought in early, asked real questions, and given space to influence what's being built.

That includes parents, students, and broader community partners. These are the people who live with the outcomes of our policies. They see the gaps. They bring perspectives that schools often miss when decisions get made in closed rooms. When families are at the table, conversations change. Policies around discipline, access to services, and communication practices start to look different.

We've seen schools rework their behavior expectations after listening to families about how discipline practices disproportionately affect their children. Others have created advisory teams that include students with IEPs and their families to review everything from class placements to extracurricular participation. These kinds of moves are hugely impactful. They help keep schools grounded in the reality of the students and families they serve. When done well, they act as checkpoints, built-in ways to make sure schools aren't drifting too far from what their communities actually need.

Students, especially those who've been marginalized, should have a say in how schools evolve. Not through token surveys, but in real decision-making roles. If we believe in student agency, then we have to design systems that actually listen to them.

When communities are part of the change, schools stop guessing what families need. They start building something together. That's how trust is built. That's how change lasts.

Scaling Without Standardizing

It's a strange thing, the way schools sometimes take a great idea and flatten it into a checklist. A flexible co-teaching model gets turned into a script with assigned lines. A new behavior framework becomes a set of laminated posters taped to every classroom wall. Before long, what started as a creative, responsive approach ends up reduced to compliance, and no one remembers why they were excited about it in the first place.

Inclusive education runs this risk more than most. Once something begins to gain traction, the pressure to "scale it up" often leads to over-defining the practice itself. On one hand it makes sense. Districts want consistency, leaders want to measure impact, and no one wants a great idea to disappear the moment someone retires or transfers. Yet when we turn inclusion into a formula, we lose the very thing that made it powerful: its adaptability.

Scaling isn't the problem. Standardizing the wrong parts is.

What we're really aiming for is shared values, not identical moves. It's the difference between developing a network and creating a franchise. A franchise expects every location to look and function the same. Same paint, same uniforms, same script. It's efficient, but it's not alive. A network, on the other hand, is built around a set of commitments. It's connected by purpose, not procedure. There's room for difference because trust has been built around the core.

Schools need to think more like networks. Teachers need room to make practices their own, to respond to the particular students in front of them. The goal isn't to lock everyone into the same approach, but to stay rooted in the purpose behind the work and give people room to figure out what that looks like in their own setting.

Here's one way to picture it. Think about a well-seasoned cast iron pan. It's durable, reliable, and capable of turning out incredible meals. But it doesn't come that way out of the box. You have to season it, layer after layer, over time. And no two pans end up exactly the same. Each one carries a history of use, a record of what's been cooked, who's done the cooking, and the choices they made in the process. That's what makes it better over time, not worse.

Scaling inclusive practices should feel like that. You start with something solid. You build it up with real use. You expect it to carry the fingerprints of the people using it. A co-teaching model should look different in a sixth-grade math class than it does in a high school humanities course. A strength-based IEP goal might sound different in a rural district than it does in an urban one. Still the underlying values of belonging, access, high expectations, relationships, those should hold steady.

There's a lot of talk in education about fidelity. Yes, it is true, fidelity is essential. But it has to be fidelity to the purpose, not to the exact procedure. You can't demand that teachers follow the letter of a practice if they're forced to ignore the spirit of it. If the goal is engagement, and the "approved" strategy leaves students disconnected and teachers frustrated, something's off.

Teachers also bring different strengths to the table. What works well for one teacher may not translate perfectly to another. Some create connection through humor, others through one-on-one check-ins. Some are visual thinkers, others lean into storytelling. If we try to iron all of that out in the name of consistency, we lose the richness that makes inclusive classrooms work in the first place.

Instead of enforcing uniformity, schools should focus on clarity. Be clear about what is important: student voice, flexible pathways, high expectations for everyone, no matter what labels are attached. Be clear about what's non-negotiable: dignity, access, and growth. Also, be just as clear about what is negotiable, so teachers aren't afraid to adjust, adapt, and refine based on what they see in front of them.

When we scale with flexibility, we're not weakening the work. We're strengthening it. We're trusting educators to bring their full selves to the job. We're recognizing that real inclusion isn't a protocol, it's a practice. And like anything worth doing, it evolves.

What we develop will never be perfect. But it can be real. It can respond. It can grow stronger over time, much like that seasoned pan, used, tested, trusted, and carried forward by the people who know how to make it work.

Real Change Is Slow and Bumpy

There's a reason schools often return to the status quo, even after big shifts. It's not always about lack of funding or even staffing. It's mindset, and when one school I worked with made the transition to fully inclusive practices, that was the first thing their director said when I asked what had been the hardest part. It wasn't the scheduling. It wasn't budgets. It was shifting beliefs. Beliefs of staff, families, and the broader community.

Because this is something we sometimes forget: schools are made up of people. Those people carry years of stories, habits, and assumptions about what school is supposed to look like. Change challenges all of that. Especially when it touches something so embedded as how we think about disability, intelligence, or who belongs where.

The push for equity is often framed as something urgent. As it should because it is. But it's also slow. It doesn't move in a straight line. There are wins and setbacks, progress and pushback, all happening at once. And at the first sign of slipping test scores or a change in leadership, equity work is often the first thing to go. It's seen as extra. Optional. Nice when everything else is running smoothly.

This is why sustainability counts. The work has to be integrated into the structure of the school, not left to individual momentum. Because as much as we need passionate teachers and brave administrators, we also need systems that don't collapse when one of them leaves.

We have to acknowledge that we're not doing this in a vacuum. The pandemic didn't only disrupt learning. It exposed how fragile some of our systems really were. It magnified inequities, widened gaps, and left students with a host of new challenges. Charity Winburn (2024) writes about this in her analysis of the Next Generation Science Standards, arguing that post-pandemic students need more than rigorous expectations. They need flexibility, motivation, and a deep sense of belonging in order to re-engage with their learning.

What Winburn's work makes clear is that motivation isn't simply a personal trait. It's shaped by systems. By how much autonomy a student has. Whether they feel competent. Whether they feel like they belong. These things aren't "nice to haves." They're essential, and too often, they're missing in the way we talk about standards, outcomes, or inclusion.

When equity gets treated like a temporary initiative or something we'll get to after scores improve, we miss the point. Equity is the path to stronger outcomes. It's what allows students to show up as their full selves and engage with learning in a way that's real. It's what lets teachers stop scrambling and start teaching in ways that actually work for the students in front of them.

The school I mentioned earlier didn't become inclusive overnight. It happened in pieces, team by team, decision by decision. There were likely moments of real tension. I imagine they had conversations that got uncomfortable, and meetings where people didn't agree. But the mindset shifted. Once that happened, everything else followed. The structure, the practices, the language. It all started to align because the foundation had moved.

That's what real change looks like. It's not always dramatic. Sometimes, it's a team refusing to write the same IEP goals as last year. Or a principal carving out time for teachers to actually review student work together, not only log grades. Or a family speaking up at a board meeting and being heard.

Change doesn't need to be flashy to be powerful. But it does need to be consistent. And it needs to be grounded in the belief that our students deserve more than a system built for convenience. They deserve one built for them.

Tools to Keep Going

Sustaining change doesn't always require sweeping reform or massive restructuring. Sometimes it takes the right habits, repeated often enough that they become part of the culture.

When inclusive practices are part of the day-to-day work of a school, not only something listed on the PD calendar, they start to take hold in real, lasting ways.

What's important here is consistency. Not perfection. Not a flashy rollout. Just tools that keep the work visible, collaborative, and responsive. The kind of things that can happen in ten minutes at the start of a team meeting, or during a hallway check-in that turns into something more meaningful.

Here are a few tools that can help teams stay grounded in what truly counts:

Quick Tools for Ongoing Inclusive Practice

Team Huddles
Keep it short, focused, and regular. A 15-minute weekly check-in where grade-level or content teams ask: Who's not fully included right now? What do we need to adjust?

Equity Audits
Pick one area: whether that is discipline referrals, advanced coursework enrollment, or reading levels, and look at the data by student group. Ask what story it's telling, and whose voices are missing from the conversation.

Inclusion Walkthroughs
Walk classrooms with a simple lens: Who's participating? Who's visible? These aren't formal evaluations. They're quick snapshots meant to guide support and prompt honest reflection. Invite educators to do them together and reflect on what they notice.

Reflective Protocols
Use structured prompts in team meetings to pause and think:

- What assumptions are showing up in how we talk about students?
- What strengths are we focusing on, and whose are they?
- What barriers did a student experience this week, and how did we respond?

Student Feedback Loops

Make space for students to share how school feels for them. This could be a weekly reflection, a rotating advisory panel, or even anonymous comment boxes. And most importantly: respond to what they say.

No single tool will transform a school. However, these small, intentional routines can keep equity from becoming invisible. They keep the focus where it belongs, which is on students. It will also remind everyone that inclusion isn't a task. It's a mindset that shows up in what we do every day.

Closing Reflection: From Heroic to Habitual

Every school has its heroes walking the halls like everyone else. You wouldn't know it at first glance, but they're the ones doing some of the most important work. The teacher who stays after a team meeting to figure out how to include a student who keeps getting overlooked. The counselor who challenges a long-standing referral process. The administrator who keeps inclusion on the agenda, even when the pressure is to pivot to something else. These moments may not look heroic from the outside, but they are. And they matter.

The goal isn't to rely on heroic effort forever. The goal is to build something that lasts when the capes come off.

Because real change doesn't happen in the dramatic moments. It happens in the daily ones. It shows up in hallway conversations, lesson plans, and staffing decisions. In who gets invited into the room and whose voices help shape the work. It happens when equity and inclusion stop being something we rally around during crises and start being the way we do school.

That shift from heroic to habitual means creating systems where the bar is set high and students are actually given what they need to reach it. So it doesn't take a superhuman effort to get kids what they need. So the next teacher, the next student, the next family doesn't have to start from scratch.

So before you close this chapter, take a minute to ask yourself (see Table 9.1).

This work isn't about being perfect. It's about being persistent. It's about building a school where every student feels

TABLE 9.1 Questions to Guide Sustainable Change

Question	Why It Matters
What would it take for this to be how we do things, not the exception?	Makes us examine whether practices are truly embedded or treated as temporary. Pushes for a culture shift, not just another short-term initiative.
Who are your co-heroes?	Reminds us that change is collective work. Identifies partners and allies already leading, so you don't stand alone.
What will you keep doing even when it gets hard?	Grounds the work in persistence. Prepares you to keep going when time, data, or resistance make things challenging.

like they have place, and where the adults believe it, too. That doesn't require superpowers. Just a shared commitment, held long enough to become culture.

Keep the cape if it reminds you why you started. That said, know it's okay to set it down sometimes. You don't have to wear it every day to make an impact.

References

Crockett, J. B. (2002). Special education's role in preparing responsive leaders for inclusive schools. *Remedial and Special Education, 23*(3), 157–168. https://doi.org/10.1177/07419325020230030401

Endrew F. v. Douglas County School District, 580 U.S. (2017). https://www.supremecourt.gov/opinions/16pdf/15-827_0pm1.pdf

National Equity Project. (2016). *Educational equity: A definition.* https://www.nationalequityproject.org/resources/educational-equity-definition

Tomlinson, C. A., & Moon, T. R. (2013). *Assessment and student success in a differentiated classroom.* ASCD.

Winburn, C. R. (2024). Meeting the needs of the individual student in the post-pandemic era: An analysis of the next generation science standards. *Cultural Studies of Science Education, 19*(1), 23–35. https://doi.org/10.1007/s11422-023-10191-2

Conclusion

The Hero's Next Mission

There's an old problem from philosophy called the Trolley Problem. It's meant to be theoretical, but it feels familiar. A train is heading toward five people. You stand at the lever. If you do nothing, those five get hit. If you pull it, one person is hit on the other track. Someone gets hurt either way. The lesson is about utilitarianism and hard choices. For educators, it likely feels routine.

Superheroes in movies get big rescues and dramatic choices. Educators don't get capes or secret gadgets. They work with the same limits as anyone else, but the stakes still feel real, and the outcomes still have consequences. That's what makes this job so hard. It's also what makes it heroic.

Working in education is full of impossible choices.

You have 28 students. One is melting down every morning. Do you stop the lesson and address it? Remove them? Ignore it to keep teaching? Five kids need your help, but one needs everything you've got, right now.

Then there's the parent who emails again, frustrated and anxious. Their child has struggled all year. You've tried scaffolding, check-ins, behavior charts, reteaching, modific ations, and you have a folder thick enough to stop a door. You care, but so do the other parents waiting for answers. What happens when helping one means falling behind for the rest?

There's the bigger stuff: policy decisions. You advocate for inclusive practices. You question removing students for behaviors that come from regulation, not rebellion. Now you're labeled a squeaky wheel. You want to change things, yet still keep your head down long enough to make it to June.

These aren't abstract ideas. They shape classrooms, hallway conversations, Individualized Education Program (IEP) meetings, and that sinking feeling when the right thing and the practical thing don't match. No one tells you that being an educator means carrying more ethical tension in a day than most people feel in a month.

Still, you show up.

While the Trolley Problem offers two choices, educators know better. You've found workarounds, noticed nuance, refused to accept that helping one child means failing another.

Somehow you figure out how to do both.

You rewrite the rules, slow the train, and question whether those tracks were ever built with all kids in mind.

That's the work.

Every student deserves support. Our role isn't to choose between them but to build systems that reach them all. More importantly, it means refusing to let that pressure change your values.

When educators feel forced to trade off inclusion for instruction, behavior for academics, or helping one for helping many, that's not poor decision-making. That signals something upstream is broken.

That shift doesn't always come from policy or a new initiative. Sometimes it comes from the small, radical decisions made by educators. Like the teacher who lets a student stand and pace instead of demanding stillness. Or the one who offers to let a student remove staples from the wall as long as he refrains from racist comments. The principal who sketches out a work-based placement so a student can show off skills instead of shutting down. The teacher who sets up makeshift kettlebells with taped-up textbooks, giving a student the heavy work he craves to steady his mind. The team that rethinks a schedule until it finally fits kids who need it most.

These are intentional choices, grounded in what kids actually need. Real resistance. Consistent persistence.

Yes, sometimes it's exhausting. There will be days when the train barrels forward anyway, and you feel like you failed. Remember those days are not the full story. They aren't the end of the chapter.

The real story is that you keep coming back, looking for better answers.

The Trolley Problem might be theoretical. Education isn't. You are not stuck at the lever. You are not alone on the tracks. You still have options.

You're the one who dares to ask, "Why are these the only choices?"

Then starts building new ones.

You Are Not Powerless

Educators face impossible situations, but you're not powerless. It might not feel that way, yet you're not simply reacting to what's thrown at you. You help guide what happens next.

That makes a difference.

We often underestimate the small decisions made in chaos. They don't come with applause or show up on staff agendas. Still, they have an impact. They change the energy and set the tone for how kids experience school.

Think about the days when you made time for a student who usually gets left out. The days you stayed a few minutes after school to check in with a kid who'd otherwise go unnoticed. The mornings you adjusted your lesson on the fly because you saw something different in your students' eyes when they walked in. These are intentional moves. Small choices rooted in care, in purpose, in knowing your students. Acts of care. And they change the dynamics in a classroom more than any policy memo ever could.

Years ago, I worked with a student named Marcus. He'd been removed from multiple classrooms. His folder read like a history book of referrals. Most believed he couldn't "do school." But when the rigid structure was lifted, and he didn't feel one mistake away from being kicked out, he was a different kid.

One teacher decided not to follow the old plan. Instead of placing him in a corner with a packet and behavior chart, she gave him a leadership role in morning meeting. She called home with positive updates. She offered him a fidget toy, even though it wasn't on his IEP. Simple, thoughtful, and designed around who Marcus actually was.

There were still hard days. Yet that teacher's classroom was the first where he wasn't removed in over a year.

Those small shifts made a big impact.

This is what it looks like to operate from a strengths-based lens. Not because it's trendy or in a PD slide deck, but because it works. Because when you choose to see students as more than their struggles, you begin to operate differently. You plan, talk to families, and build systems with more hope.

When multiple educators do that, things start to change.

This isn't about martyrdom or glorifying burnout. You aren't the system, but you have influence. Real influence. You are why some kids return the next day. Why some families feel heard. Why some students believe they can do hard things.

That's not a small thing.

And yet, it's so easy to forget that when you're caught in the day-to-day scramble. You're managing behaviors, balancing academic pressures, trying to comply with documentation requirements that never seem to end. The exhaustion is real, as is the isolation, but so is your power.

You don't need to move mountains. Keep moving one rock at a time. That's how pathways open. That's how new routes get made.

If it feels like no one's noticing, remember your students are. Even the ones who don't say it or resist every bit of support still feel it. That connection stays with them long after they leave your classroom.

The system is flawed at times. Expectations can feel impossible. Some days leave you wondering why you ever signed up for this.

Then you remember: you are not powerless.

You build something better, one decision at a time.

The Language We Use Shapes the Path We Choose

There's a phrase you hear across helping professions: "meet them where they are." I get the intent, I really do. It reminds us to accept students as they are, to honor their starting points. Still, I've always had trouble with that phrase.

Meeting a student where they are cannot be the end goal.

Some of our students face hard circumstances: trauma, chaos, or home lives more complex than most people realize. We need to understand and respond to those realities, yet we cannot stay stuck there. They deserve more. They deserve educators who will walk with them and help them move forward.

Pulling up a chair beside a student's struggle isn't enough. At some point, we have to say, "I see where you are, and I believe you can go further." When that belief is genuine, it changes everything: how we design instruction, how we respond to behavior, and how we see potential.

That brings us to something we rarely say enough: language makes a difference.

What we say about students builds the framework around them. It impacts how we respond, how we talk with families, and how we define growth. Calling a student "non-compliant" signals one kind of response; describing them as "struggling with regulation today" invites another. Our language shows how much room we make for growth.

We often claim a strengths-based lens, yet still describe students almost entirely by what they can't do. He's low. She's behind. They don't have the skills. That language becomes a filter. When it passes from teacher to teacher, grade to grade, it starts to stick. The student hears it. The family feels it. Eventually, it frames what the student believes about themselves.

We have to be careful.

This isn't about ignoring struggle or pretending things are easier than they are. It means telling the whole story: hard parts and hopeful parts. Every student has strengths. Every student brings something. If we're not sure what that is yet, our job is to keep looking instead of filling in assumptions.

I've been in too many meetings where a student's challenges take up 90% of the talk, with a quick, "But he's really sweet," or "She tries hard." What if we flipped that ratio? Led with what's working, what excites them, where they've grown? That grounds the conversation in possibility instead of pathology.

Even the way we talk about services and supports guides what happens next. We say things like, "He's being pulled for resource," or "She's only on a 504." We talk about students "qualifying" for help, as though it's some exclusive club instead of a basic part of access. Sometimes interventions even get framed as punishments: "If he keeps this up, he'll end up in the behavior room."

Kids hear that. They absorb it. They start to internalize the idea that support means something is wrong with them.

We have to change that. Not only in policy documents, but in everyday conversations. In team meetings. In emails. In the way we describe our students to one another and to ourselves.

Language influences direction. What we say about students doesn't only stay in the staff room. It makes its way into how we work with them and what we believe is possible for them.

How we talk about kids directs how we show up for them.

So let's talk like we believe in their capacity to grow. Let's talk like we expect them to succeed. Let's talk like our words have weight. Because they do.

The Cost of Caring

There was a student we worked with for years. His name was Anthony.

We knew him well. We'd been in meetings together, sat with his teachers, and talked with his caregiver more times than I can count. He was part of our community. He wasn't always easy or predictable, yet he was no stranger to any of us.

One day, without warning, we got a call from a neighboring district. He'd moved and enrolled there. They had questions and wanted some background. We had no idea he was gone. No notice, no transition meeting, no chance to say goodbye. He was simply gone.

When we finally reached his guardian, they explained what happened. Things at home had reached a breaking point. His behavior had spiraled. They couldn't manage anymore. The situation had fallen apart.

In school, though, he'd been doing okay. Not perfect, but stable. Safe. Regulated most days. Whatever was happening at home hadn't shown up in our building yet. We didn't see it coming.

After that call, we sat there. It wasn't the usual silence of waiting to speak. It was the kind that comes when you're holding something you can't fully process, trying to make sense of it. I kept turning over the same questions: Did we miss something? Was there more we could have done? Would it have changed anything?

That's the part people don't always talk about.

You can do everything right. Build the plan, adjust the environment, keep showing up. And still, it can slip. Not for lack of caring. Not for lack of effort. Sometimes, despite everything you pour into a child, you don't get to control the outcome.

And it hurts.

You wonder what might have happened if things played out differently. You wonder if any of it mattered.

Here's what I've come to believe: it did.

Those years of support, structure, and connection meant something. Even if we didn't see the long-term result. Even if he left and things fell apart later. For that stretch of time, Anthony had consistency. He had people who believed in him, who greeted him without judgment, who saw more than his behaviors. That doesn't disappear just because the story changed.

We don't always get closure. We build moments that stay. We show students what it feels like to be known and cared for. That effort, even when offered without any guarantee of success, is what working in education is really about.

Not every story ends the way we hope. Not every student we invest in leaves us stronger. Still, we don't stop trying, because the trying itself is the point.

So we keep showing up, even when we're tired or unsure it's working. That steady, imperfect, relentless effort is what moves this work forward. One student at a time. One day at a time.

An Invitation Forward

If you've made it this far, then hopefully something here felt familiar. Perhaps, it named what you've been feeling but couldn't quite put into words. Maybe it reminded you that you're not the only one trying to do impossible things every day, without a cape or a secret gadget, while juggling paperwork, behaviors, IEPs, and the crowded schedule before lunch.

It's okay to admit that working in education is hard. Full of contradictions and trade-offs. Moments where you wonder if what you're doing makes a difference. Still, here's what stays true: you are not simply surviving this system. You're reshaping it. Every time you challenge a deficit narrative. Every time you make a decision based on a student's real needs, not only what the form says. Every time you build trust with a family or keep showing up for a student others have given up on. That is what change looks like. It won't grab headlines or happen overnight, but it makes a difference.

You don't need to have it all figured out. You only need to keep choosing work that centers kids. The kind that says: you belong here. You valued here. I haven't given up on you. The kind that tells your students that, and maybe, on some days, tells you too.

What comes next won't be perfect. There will still be tension between what you want to do and what the system allows. The question to remember is not "How do I fix everything?" but "What kind of educator do I want to be, even in the middle of uncertainty?"

We won't create equity through compliance. We won't build inclusion through isolation. We get there by listening harder. By speaking up. By seeing each student as a person first, and making choices that honor who they are, even when it's inconvenient.

Working in education isn't the kind of work that gets tied up with a bow. Maybe that's the point.

Because the real work is the kind that stays. It changes lives. It doesn't live in a new initiative or a binder on a shelf. It lives in the daily, sometimes invisible, always powerful choice to show up and keep going.

So consider this your invitation:

Keep asking hard questions, assuming less, speaking up, and staying curious. Push back when needed, hold the line when it counts, and keep trying even when the outcome is uncertain.

Tell a new story.

For your students. For your school. Maybe even for yourself.

If there is one thing I hope you carry forward from these pages, it's this: what you do matters.

More than you know.

For Product Safety Concerns and Information please contact our EU
representative GPSR@taylorandfrancis.com
Taylor & Francis Verlag GmbH, Kaufingerstraße 24, 80331 München, Germany

www.ingramcontent.com/pod-product-compliance
Lightning Source LLC
Chambersburg PA
CBHW070403240426
43661CB00056B/2512